Jesus – Opening Our Hearts

The Christian Aid/Hodder Lent Book 2004

Edited by Paula Clifford

Hodder & Stoughton

LONDON SYDNEY AUCKLAND

Copyright © 2003 by Christian Aid

First published in Great Britain in 2003

The right of Christian Aid to be identified as the Author of
the Work has been asserted by them in accordance with
the Copyright, Designs and Patents Act 1988.

10 9 8 7 6 5 4 3 2 1

British Library Cataloguing in Publication Data
A record for this book is available from the British Library

ISBN 0 340 78718 X

Typeset in Garamond by Avon DataSet Ltd, Bidford-on-Avon, Warwickshire

Printed and bound in Great Britain by
Bookmarque Ltd, Croydon, Surrey

The paper and board used in this paperback are natural recyclable products
made from wood grown in sustainable forests. The manufacturing processes
conform to the environmental regulations of the country of origin.

Hodder & Stoughton
A Division of Hodder Headline Ltd
338 Euston Road
London NW1 3BH
www.madaboutbooks.com

Contents

Contributors

Mary Bradford is Senior Campaigns Officer for Christian Aid, with responsibility for developing and overseeing campaigning with and through the churches. She is a member of the Church of England and has travelled extensively in India and West Africa.

Wendy Bray is a freelance writer and journalist, with a special interest in family and faith issues. Originally a teacher, she worked until recently with Care for the Family as staff writer. Wendy's first book, *In the Palm of God's Hand* (Bible Reading Fellowship), was a winner in the Christian Book Awards 2002. She and her family belong to Mutley Baptist Church in Devon.

Lavinia Byrne is a writer and religious commentator. She taught communications in the Cambridge Theological Federation for six years after working at the Council of Churches for Britain and Ireland. Her books include *The Journey is My Home* (Hodder, 2000).

Paula Clifford is writer and publications manager for Christian Aid in London, and a Church of England Lay Reader in the Oxford Diocese. She is a former academic and has published books on a wide range of topics. Her next book is a study of Catherine of Siena.

Andrew McLellan is Her Majesty's Chief Inspector of Prisons for Scotland. He is a minister of the Church of Scotland; he was Moderator of the General Assembly of 2000 and as Moderator visited development projects in many countries. He was until 2002 minister of St Andrew's and St George's in Edinburgh where the annual book sale has raised over £1 million for Christian Aid.

Njongonkulu Ndungane is Archbishop of Cape Town. He is the son and grandson of Anglican clergy in South Africa and discovered his own vocation to the priesthood while in prison on Robben Island during the apartheid regime. A popular speaker and broadcaster, the Archbishop is a patron of Jubilee 2000 and is currently playing a leading role in the campaign against HIV/AIDS. He is the author of *A World with a Human Face: A Voice from Africa* (SPCK, 2003).

Chris Sugden is Executive Director of the Oxford Centre for Mission Studies, a trustee of Traidcraft and a Canon of St Luke's Cathedral, Jos, Nigeria. He is married to Elaine, a cancer consultant, and they have three adult children.

Introduction

Rapid advances in communications technology in recent years have, for better or worse, transformed our world. For many people in developed countries, the idea of a global village is very much a reality, as the old barriers of time and space are being increasingly overcome. In no time at all you can send information across vast distances, transport people or goods around the world, and set up businesses in every continent.

This transformation has overshadowed a more subtle change, which is change to our relationships: who or what we relate to, and how we do it. Relationships that we all enter into, to a greater or lesser extent, are continually changing. Take, for example, the people we may never have met but whose cause we want to espouse. Once these might have been people who suffered under the apartheid regime in South Africa or under Communist rule in eastern Europe. Today they may be refugees from Afghanistan or Iraq, or people whose lives are blighted by international debt or unfair trade rules. And because, as Christians, we are in relationship with churches around the world, their changing circumstances must also lead us to reflect on the responsibilities and demands our ecumenical relationship with them places upon us.

At a personal level, many relationships have become more complex. Family structures now frequently extend to include step-parents and step-children, as well as families of absent parents. On the other hand, in countries worst affected by the spread of HIV/AIDS, family structures have contracted, as increasing numbers of orphans are brought up by aunts and uncles or grandparents.

This book offers a variety of perspectives on human relationships and on people's relationship with God. The Archbishop of Cape Town introduces the concept of mutual dependency, *Ubuntu* (page 25), meaning 'I cannot be a whole person without you nor can you without me'. By contrast Andrew McLellan, Scotland's Chief Inspector of Prisons, writes of the devastating effects of the breakdown in relationships and refers to prisons as 'perhaps the most painful places in the land' (page 76). Yet even there some prisoners experience the reality of a new relationship with God.

The daily readings are taken mainly from the Gospel of Luke, along with a few from its 'sequel', the Acts of the Apostles. In addition most weeks begin with one or more readings from Deuteronomy, in order to highlight the Old Testament roots of much Christian thinking on relationships.

The relationships of which we are conscious of being a part will also affect, however subtly, our relationship with God. The short prayers that follow the daily reflections are intended to help express what is often so hard to put into words: our concern for people whose names we don't know and whose lives are very different from our own. As we move towards Easter we shall find there are more and more people for whom we want to pray the prayer of the penitent thief: 'Jesus, remember me when you come into your kingdom' (Luke 23:42) and with whom we shall rejoice at the words of the angel: 'He is not here; he has risen' (Luke 24:6).

Paula Clifford

Using this book in small groups

Jesus – Opening Our Hearts may be used as a basis for Lent studies by small groups meeting on a weekly basis. A suggested way of doing this is to take one of the passages from St Luke's Gospel used during the week together with a related Old Testament reading, not necessarily one which features in the reflections in this book. These will form the basis for the group's discussion and prayer week by week. Members of the group should be encouraged to use the book each day at home as well, so that they can also bring their personal reflections on other passages and related themes to the group meeting.

The following outline assumes that groups are meeting weekly, beginning in the week of Ash Wednesday. There is no study suggested for Holy Week, though some groups might choose to hold their own informal service or house communion then. In that case the Gospel reading could be the passage in the book chosen for that day.

Group leaders will probably need to examine the passages in more depth with the help of a biblical commentary, in order to help the group with questions of context and interpretation. The questions suggested for discussion may be modified or developed to fit the interests of the group. In each session a significant amount of time should be set aside for prayer or quiet meditation.

Session 1: Jesus – opening our hearts

Luke 4:1–13: Opening our hearts in solitude

Additional reading: Psalm 91

Summary
Full of the Holy Spirit, Jesus spends time alone in the wilderness, preparing for ministry yet at the same time vulnerable to temptation. Setting aside time for quiet reflection carries the same risk for us: a chance to be alone with God is also an opportunity for the devil to tempt us to aspire to wrong ambitions or to choose an easy option.

Suggested activity
Ask group members to reflect either singly or in pairs on their experience of being alone with God. Encourage them to tell the group about it and what the risks and positive benefits have been.

Questions for group discussion arising out of the Gospel passage
1 Consider each temptation in turn. What might be the equivalent (a) for your church and (b) for you personally?
2 Look at Psalm 91. How is the devil misusing Scripture when he quotes from it?
3 The devil left Jesus 'until an opportune time'. When do you think he returned? How did Jesus resist him? What can we learn from that?

For prayer, using Psalm 91
• Read verses 1–2: pray for a deeper trust in God.
• Read verses 3–8: pray for people caught up in war; pray for those who are sick or fearful. Name people and places on your heart. Pray for people who are in special need of God's protection.

- Read verses 9–16: give thanks for God's promise of love and of safekeeping. Pray that you may offer such love to those in need around you.

Session 2: Opening our hearts to people around us

Luke 18:1–8: Justice and prayer

Additional reading: Deuteronomy 4:1–8

Summary
A judge who rejects the double command that dates back to Moses – to fear God and care for one's neighbour – is worn down by the persistence of a wronged widow. His response springs from self-interest, but God's justice, freely given in response to prayer, is given out of love.

Suggested activity
Think together about persistence. This could involve looking through a current newspaper or watching some of the TV news together. Who has been persistent and in what cause? Is persistence valued? When is it not valued? Now read the verses from Luke and consider how the widow might be viewed today.

Questions for group discussion arising out of the Gospel passage
1 What do you think is the relation between justice and prayer? (Look also at Deuteronomy 4:7–8.)
2 What justice issues should we be praying about? How can we do that better?
3 The people of Israel are referred to as God's 'chosen ones' in the Old Testament only once things start to go badly for them.

Why do you think this is? How is this reflected in the teaching of Jesus?

For prayer

- *'This great nation is a wise and understanding people'*: pray for people from whom wisdom and understanding is expected: government ministers, MPs, judges and other key figures. Pray that they may show a genuine concern for justice for those in need.
- *'Will not God bring about justice for his chosen ones, who cry out to him day and night?'* Pray that we may all be faithful not only in avoiding wrong actions but also in taking positive action – praying for people in need of justice and persisting in doing whatever we can to support them.
- Pray for people or groups locally who are being treated unjustly: refugees and asylum seekers, ethnic minorities, individuals known to you. Continue to pray for them in the coming weeks.

Session 3: Opening our hearts to people in need

Luke 9:10–17: Feeding the crowds

Additional reading: Deuteronomy 19:1–7

Summary

Jesus is interrupted by crowds of people while he is alone with his disciples. And because the people are in such need of his teaching he has compassion on them (Mark 6:34) and answers their need. In turn Jesus expects the disciples to meet the people's need for food and responds to their efforts to find some with a great feeding miracle.

Suggested activity and discussion

Read the passage from Luke together. Then divide into pairs. One person imagines that he or she is one of the disciples who is with Jesus and the other that he or she is one of the crowd. Describe your feelings to each other at each point in the story: how do you feel, as a disciple, when your special time with Jesus is disturbed? What do you feel about being expected to feed the crowds? What drives the person in the crowd to seek out Jesus? How do you feel as the day wears on? What is the reaction of both of you when five thousand are fed? Ask one or more of the pairs to relay their thoughts to the whole group. Sum up what it feels like to be the person in need and the feelings you have in responding to their need.

Further question for discussion on the Gospel passage

The Archbishop of Cape Town writes (p. 29): 'There is one refuge which cannot be overlooked or ignored. That is Jesus.' In what way is Jesus shown to be a refuge in Luke 9:10–17 for the disciples and for the crowds? How may we understand him to be our refuge?

For prayer

- Reflect on the people who we are called to feed. Name them and pray for them.
- Pray for people who seek a refuge because they fear for their lives, among them battered women, abused children and political refugees. Ask that the church may be faithful in showing them the love of Jesus, our refuge.
- Pray for ourselves, that we may open our eyes to people in need and respond accordingly.

Session 4: Opening our hearts to people of faith

Luke 7:36–50: God's forgiven people

Additional reading: Psalm 51:1–17

Summary
When Simon the Pharisee objects to an unnamed woman welcoming Jesus more extravagantly than he has, Jesus responds with the story of two debtors. While the story explains the degree of love felt by those who have been forgiven much, the whole episode is a lesson to Jesus' forgiven followers about welcoming people whom God has forgiven still more.

Suggested activity
Divide the group in two. Ask one group to look at 2 Samuel 12:1–14 and the other group to focus on the Luke passage. What do we learn about forgiveness? Then discuss together the differences between the two passages.

Further questions for group discussion
What do we find it particularly hard to forgive as a Christian community? Is our attitude changed when a person believes God has forgiven them? If not, why not? How might we become a more forgiving church?

For prayer, using Psalm 51
- Read verses 1–6: give thanks for God's compassion and mercy on his sinful people; pray that we may be more accepting of people who know they have been forgiven by him but who meet with an unforgiving attitude from their church or community.
- Read verses 7–9: pray for forgiveness for ourselves, our church, our nation.

- Read verses 10–12: pray that as forgiven Christians we may show the joy of the psalmist and the extravagant love of the sinful woman in Luke 7.
- Read verses 13–17: ask that we may offer a genuine welcome to new Christians and recognise the special gifts that God has given them.

Session 5: Opening our hearts to family

Luke 8:19–21: The wider family

Additional reading: Deuteronomy 6:1–9

Summary

In an apparently harsh aside, Jesus rejects the idea that 'family' in a Christian sense is to be limited to our blood relatives. In so doing he also makes it clear that no person or group has an exclusive relationship with him.

Suggested activity

Invite group members to bring to the meeting a photo of either a member of their family or someone who is a close friend. Put all the photos together in a pile and ask people to choose a photo that someone else has brought. Then take it in turns to tell the group something about the person featured in your original photo. Finally, either in silence or aloud, pray for the person in the photo that you now have in the light of what you have learnt about them.

(The group will need advance warning of this. The leader should also have a couple of spare photos, perhaps of people from another part of the world, which can be used if group members have forgotten to bring a photo of their own.)

Questions for group discussion

1 In Mark's account of this incident Jesus asks the question: 'Who are my mother and my brothers?' (Mark 3:33). How are we to answer that question? What implications do our answers have for our prayers and actions?

2 'Only in their own towns, among their relatives and in their own homes are prophets without honour' (Mark 6:4, NIV Inclusive). Why is it so difficult to talk about our faith to those who know us best?

3 How can we really regard people we've never met as our family?

For prayer

• 'Impress [these commandments] on your children' (Deuteronomy 6:7). Pray for the children's work of your church, for the young people who come and for those who lead them.

• Pray for young people with problems, especially any known to you personally. Ask that God will use you and others to befriend and help them, and pray for courage to do it effectively.

• Pray for another Christian community either nearby or overseas. Continue to pray for them in the coming weeks.

Session 6: Opening our hearts to suffering

Luke 7:11–17: A grieving mother

Additional reading: 1 Kings 17:17–24

Summary

Like Elijah before him, Jesus responds to the death of a widow's son by bringing him back to life, and is likewise acclaimed as a great prophet. But unlike Elijah, Jesus is clearly stated to be motivated by compassion, and this will eventually lead him to experience for himself the most intense human suffering.

Suggested activity

In the Gospels women are frequently shown to be suffering and inviting Jesus' compassion. They include the woman with a flow of blood, the woman caught in adultery, Martha and Mary at the time of Lazarus' death and Jesus' mother at the cross. Divide into twos or threes and ask each small group to reflect on one of these women, putting themselves in her position. Then feed back to the whole group, not for debate but in the form of a reflection, what it feels like for a vulnerable and suffering woman to experience Jesus' compassion.

Questions for group discussion on the Gospel passage

1 What are the significant differences between Jesus' healing miracle and that of Elijah in 1 Kings 17? How do these differences point to Jesus being the Son of God?

2 Think about the other occasions when Jesus raises someone from the dead – Jairus' daughter (Luke 8), Lazarus (John 11). What details do all three miracles have in common? What purpose does each one serve in the overall Gospel narrative?

For prayer

• Pray for people in prison and those who weep for them outside.

• 'When the Lord saw her, his heart went out to her.' Pray that as a church and as individuals we may show greater compassion to those who suffer, particularly to people such as the mentally ill whose suffering often passes unnoticed.

• Give thanks for God's power over suffering; pray that this message of hope may be widely heard this Passiontide.

Jesus – Opening Our Hearts

Day 1: Ash Wednesday

INTRODUCTION:
JESUS – OPENING OUR HEARTS

PAULA CLIFFORD

Opening our hearts in solitude
Luke 4:1–13

He will command his angels . . . to guard you carefully.
(Luke 4:10)

Being alone is a challenging experience, and one which affects different people in different ways. It can alter ways of thinking and behaving; it can make or break relationships. Few people emerge unchanged from a period of solitude. Perhaps because of this, since the first centuries of the Christian era, holy men and women have deliberately withdrawn from society to deepen their relationship with God. Although the manner in which some of them once lived – in the wide open spaces of the desert, or cooped up in small cells – may seem to us to be almost unendurable, this has led, among other things, to some of the greatest works of Christian spirituality. The solitude of a few has been to the inestimable benefit of many.

But while the wilderness may be a creative place it is also a dangerous one. The mind plays tricks on you, there's no one around to straighten out your thinking or to provide a sense of proportion. You're vulnerable. What seems like space to be alone with God is also an invitation to the devil to fill the void. And Jesus certainly needed the careful protection of God's angels during his wilderness period.

Jesus' wilderness was not somewhere distant or exotic – it was right there on his doorstep. And so it will be for us. We don't need to travel the world to find God. I cannot pretend to have found spiritual insights while gazing at the vast expanse of the Sahara or journeying through the scrub of the Kalahari. But a half-empty church, a public park and even a crowded railway compartment are all places where God has spoken to me when my heart was quiet. In his short book *The Desert in the City* (HarperCollins) Carlo Carretto expresses this simple truth: the desert isn't necessarily characterised by the absence of human beings, but rather by the presence of God.

The decision to use the period of Lent to reflect on our relationships with other people and to deepen our relationship with God may be both a creative and a dangerous one. And we need to commit these weeks to God at the outset, seeking the guidance of the Holy Spirit as our reflections lead us into fresh awareness of him and of those around us.

Lord God we pray this Lent that you will command your angels to guard us carefully. May we not be tempted to pursue new spiritual experiences in our own strength and on our own initiative, but find comfort in your presence and guidance through your word.

Day 2

Opening our hearts to God's word
Luke 4:14–30

Today this scripture is fulfilled in your hearing. (Luke 4:21)

Jesus' period alone in the desert was limited. His deepened relationship with God which must surely have followed from his refusal to engage in any kind of relationship with the devil was his preparation for a gruelling three-year ministry. And for all its hardships the wilderness may have become a difficult place to leave. That was the experience of a sixth-century hermit, John Climacus, who spent forty years living in solitude at the foot of Mount Sinai. Then he was called by God to a completely different way of life – to become the head of a nearby monastic community.

John Climacus was called out of solitude to proclaim and live out the word of God. So too Jesus, in his first public appearance recorded by Luke after the forty days in the wilderness, goes to the synagogue to read the Scriptures. But the teaching that Jesus draws from them is something no one had ever heard before. 'Today,' he says, 'this Scripture is fulfilled in your hearing' (v. 21). His listeners really would have to open their hearts and their minds to make sense of this claim by the son of the local carpenter and to understand how he could bring 'good news to the poor'.

It is always humbling to meet people who have given up a way of life they are comfortable with to respond to a very different challenge. In the Democratic Republic of Congo I met a remarkable Italian doctor, then aged eighty-two, called Laura Perna. When she retired from academic life, Dr Perna left Europe to live in a remote rural area some miles from Kinshasa. There, despite few resources and only an intermittent water supply, she set up the Kimbondo Children's Hospital for sick and abandoned children. Her courageous change in lifestyle has become a living proclamation of the good news of the gospel to those around her as well as to her many supporters back in Europe.

Even though Jesus had done the right thing in rejecting the devil's temptations to seek fame and fortune the easy way, things did not go well for him once he left the desert. His revolutionary teaching in the synagogue caused fury and put him in physical danger. Back in the world Jesus would need as never before the power of the Holy Spirit that was his Father's gift.

> 'To cultivate virtue is hard, and we can often feel burdened by the demands that virtue makes of us. But a moment comes when the sense of burden lifts, and a flame of joy lights in our hearts' (John Climacus).[1] Lord God, give us fresh courage to serve you wherever you want us to be and fill us with your Holy Spirit.

Day 3

Opening our hearts to the poor and the rich
Luke 6:17–26

*Blessed are you who are poor, for yours is
the kingdom of God. (Luke 6:20)*

Unlike Matthew, Luke sets Jesus' Sermon on the Mount in the
context of healing. In this Gospel, Jesus' teaching comes
across as a direct result of his encounter with people in greatest
need. So the disciples are taught why they should follow his example
in opening their hearts to people who are most in need of healing
and compassion: because it is they who will receive blessing in God's
kingdom.

Probably it wasn't an easy lesson for the disciples to learn, any
more than it is for us: that relationships that reflect a Christ-like
love will bring us into contact with people whose situations are very
different from our own; that such relationships may well place
demands on us that, given the choice, we might prefer not to meet.

In Mytkyina in northern Burma a sixty-eight-year-old man called
Zung Pawm is one of eight generations of his family to practise
traditional medicine. But unlike his forefathers, Zung Pawm has
found himself confronted with people showing symptoms of HIV.
He experimented with various herbal remedies to help their suffering and became remarkably successful in improving their general
health. Now, in return for his services, Zung Pawm only charges
what people can afford, and many of them are subsidised by the
Myanmar Council of Churches. He comments, 'This is not a
business, the aim is especially to help the poor.' Zung Pawm has
rejected approaches from commercial companies because he knows

that if he markets his remedies the poor will suffer. He sums it all up in these words: 'The Bible says "Blessed are the poor" . . . and my ministry is with the poor.'

For this man, ministering to the poor has meant taking the trouble to learn about a new disease and work out the most helpful medication. It has meant giving up some of the income to which he might well have felt he was entitled. But this has not been at the expense of the rich. Zung Pawm cares for them too. He has opened his heart to people in need around him, but he has given most to those who are weakest.

'I will search for the lost and bring back the strays. I will bind up the injured and strengthen the weak' (Ezekiel 34:16). Thank you, God, for your promise to care for those who are weak. May we never flinch from the efforts that might be demanded of us when we seek to follow your example.

Day 4

Opening our hearts to love
Luke 24:25–32

Were not our hearts burning within us while he talked with us on the road? (Luke 24:32)

For the disciples making their way to Emmaus, hearing Jesus explain how all the Scriptures pointed to him seems to have sent shivers down their spines – a feeling that everything was falling into place. Suddenly what had seemed destructive and irrational – the brutal end to the work of a loving healer and patient teacher – began to make perfect sense. They began to understand how the love for all people which they'd seen in action during Jesus' ministry had to result in his death if humankind was to know fullness of life.

However we might describe that feeling – a tingling in the spine, a burning in the heart – it's one which most Christians are familiar with. It may well be associated with understanding: a flash of insight, such as that experienced by the disciples. Or it may be the sudden realisation that a prayer has been answered, or the result of an encounter with God. Or it may simply be that we are witnessing an example of Christ-like love in action.

A couple of years ago I met an Indian man who, like the rest of his family, was a bonded labourer. His young son had just been rescued from hard labour in a brick kiln by the South Asia Coalition for Child Servitude. The boy had been taken to a home in the country where he could enjoy his childhood and learn some basic skills, and this was his father's first visit. He was overwhelmed by what he saw. He told me, 'I've never known anyone want to help poor people without getting anything out of it for themselves. Now

I will tell hundreds of thousands of people that I have seen a miracle.'

This, surely, is the miracle of love. Opening our hearts to loving other people means putting their interests, their safety, before our own. There are too many people in the developing world who have only experienced people willing to help the poor simply because of what they themselves can get out of it. There are too many people who have known only the self-interest of the bad shepherds of Ezekiel 34 and not the love of the Good Shepherd of John 10. Yet when we see such love being extended to the unloved, then do not also our hearts burn within us?

Lord Jesus, we pray that we may never cease to marvel at revelations of your love and of your presence in our lives. Fill our hearts with love this Lent, that we may become better witnesses to the truth of your love for all people. May we not put our own interests first but engage willingly with those around us, for what may seem routine to us may be no less than a miracle to others.

Day 5

WEEK 1: OPENING OUR HEARTS
TO PEOPLE AROUND US

MARY BRADFORD

God's wise and understanding people
Deuteronomy 4:1–8

What other nation . . . [has] such righteous
decrees and laws? (Deuteronomy 4:8)

After forty years of wandering in the wilderness, the people of Israel pause on the edge of the long-promised land. Moses, who has led them through the wilderness but knows that he will not cross the Jordan himself, gives a final extended sermon on how they are to build their society in the new land.

They must observe the laws which have been given by God. The rule of God must be at the heart of their national life. We shall see later in Deuteronomy some of the aspects of that law that inspire the struggle for justice today – care for the poorest and special treatment for those who are marginalised.

So how can we advocate for God's rule in our own national life today? What are the values that will make us 'a wise and understanding people'? Perhaps most of all it is to open our hearts to those around us, and particularly to the poor, the weak and the marginalised. Sin closes our eyes to anyone who is not 'like me'. God opens them to enable us to find his image in all people.

On the agenda of my recent church council meeting was the issue of access to our historic parish church for people with disabilities. Under new government legislation we are required to make any alterations necessary. 'More red tape, more money to be spent, and for heaven's sake we don't even have any disabled people at our church!' That could so easily have been the tone of the discussion. But thankfully it was also an opportunity to reflect on how we could ensure everyone was welcome in our church community. Sometimes government policy can help to bring the kingdom closer!

On 19 June 2002, more than 13,000 people gathered in the early summer sunshine outside Westminster to lobby their Members of Parliament as part of the growing campaign for trade justice for the world's poorest countries. One MP, John Barrett, commented, 'People outside are not asking for a better deal for themselves. They are saying, "Give the poorest of the poor and the hungry and the starving of the world a fair deal – let them have a chance to help themselves, and end a trading system that kicks people when they are down." '

Lord God, you hold the nations of the world in your hands. Guide us as we take part in our national life.

Help us to open our hearts to people around us, and to use our voices and our votes to make their needs heard, so that our nation may be valued as a 'wise and understanding people'.

Day 6

Cancelling debt
Deuteronomy 15:1–11

At the end of every seven years you must cancel debts.
(Deuteronomy 15:1)

Before about 1997, this must have been one of the more obscure passages of the Bible, familiar only to erudite Old Testament scholars and the most devout of Bible-based Christians. Yet it became an inspiration for one of the biggest mass campaigns of the twentieth century: the Jubilee 2000 campaign for debt cancellation.

It forms part of Moses' 'sermon' as the people of Israel waited on the edge of the promised land and it suggests a radical new way of doing economics. Every seven years all debts incurred are to be cancelled. In other words, it is impossible for one person to accumulate capital from another. But this does not mean that money shouldn't be lent: verses 8 and 9 show a very real understanding of human nature – or what economists would call market forces!

Scholars tell us that it is unclear whether this 'jubilee' principle (named after the 'jubilee' or fiftieth year) was ever put into practice. Modern economists might argue that such a system, with no long-term incentive for the creditor, would never work.

But its underlying principle still inspired many. Twenty-four million people signed the Jubilee 2000 petition for debt cancellation for the poorest countries. Hundreds of thousands gathered at demonstrations across the world. And although the debt cancellation which resulted was more a grudging recognition of economic reality than the open-hearted gesture campaigners had hoped for, debt was cancelled.

At the time of writing, £27.5 billion has been wiped off the books for some of the poorest countries in the world: Uganda, Bolivia, Mozambique, Mali – and more. It's not enough, but it's still real progress. Children are going to school, clinics are being opened, roads are being repaired.

Perhaps the greatest achievement of the campaign was to provide a practical opportunity for ordinary Christians and others to open their hearts to people living in poverty. Jubilee 2000 gave the churches something to be proud of and changed the lives of many in this country. As Daleep Mukarji, Director of Christian Aid, said in 2000, 'Tens of thousands of church people have discovered that they can make a real difference to issues of international debt and global poverty.'

For all that, we give thanks to God.

Lord God, your Spirit was at work in the Jubilee 2000 campaign, energising, inspiring and encouraging campaigners throughout the world. We give you thanks for all that has been achieved, and we ask for your continued inspiration and wisdom to build on what has been done and to work for a fairer and more just world.

Day 7

*Do not take advantage of a hired man who is
poor and needy. (Deuteronomy 24:14)*

Opening our hearts to people around us, and particularly to
those who are poor, was central to the way God wanted the
people of Israel to behave. This passage outlines some very specific
commands and a simple underlying principle.

The specific commands recognise that one of the greatest
problems facing poor people is lack of long-term financial security.
A poor man borrows money and all he has to give as security for the
loan is his one cloak. So, Moses says, you must return his cloak at
night – and he will bless you. Hired labourers rely on receiving
their wages each day – they have nothing to fall back on. The reality
of such insecurity is as true now as it was at the time of Moses – in
India alone there are estimated to be over a hundred million
labourers with no land of their own. And the poorest and most
marginalised groups of people are still likely to be those identified
in verse 20: 'the alien, the fatherless and the widow'.

But how are we to respond today? The underlying principle of
this passage is clear but challenging: the degree to which we seek
justice for the poor is a measure of a right relationship with God.
God regards as righteous those actions for which the poor are
thankful (v. 13). Conversely, when a poor person cries out, the one
who is taking advantage of him or her is guilty of sin (v. 15). As
Michael Taylor has put it, 'the validity of what we believe [is linked]
to its fruitfulness in promoting change in favour of the poorest'.[2]

So can these verses inspire us to look at our own response to the economic structures which oppress the poor today? Are we able to do something, for which the poor will one day bless us? The Bible urges practical action – and there are things we can do.

Perhaps this Lent you could add your voice to the growing Trade Justice campaign. Christian Aid is campaigning with many churches and other organisations for radical change to the way international trade works. Trade could be a way out of poverty for millions – but at the moment it is only making things worse. The campaign is calling for international trade rules to be weighted in favour of poor people: the vision of Moses is still alive today.

Lord God, you love and want the best for all your children, but particularly for the poor, the outcast and the powerless. Give us inspiration to share your love, and to do what we can to change the world so that the needs of the poor come first.

Day 8

Praying for justice
Luke 18:1–8

Will not God bring about justice for his chosen ones . . . ?
(Luke 18:7)

What a fantastic campaigner! This story has such a ring of truth to it that it's hard not to believe that Jesus had a particular incident in mind when he told this parable. Here was a woman who just wouldn't give up. She knew her cause was right, and she was determined to get justice. Like campaigners today she knew that people can be persuaded in many ways, but not least by sheer dogged persistence!

Reading this passage with modern eyes we can be tempted to think of this woman as just 'a bit of a nag' – the kind of irritating person who is always on about something. But Jesus makes it clear that justice was on her side. First of all, it's stated that she was a widow, which to Jesus' listeners would have immediately character-ised her as one of those singled out for special treatment in the Jewish law. Second, the judge's attitude is summed up in the words: '[he] neither feared God nor cared about men'. Even-handed justice for the poor, and particularly for widows, orphans and foreigners, was a basic legal tenet (Exodus 23:6, Deuteronomy 27:19), which this judge blatantly ignored.

Luke tells us that this parable was told to show the disciples that 'they should always pray and not give up'. But does that mean we should see God as some kind of reluctant official, who will give in to our demands only when we mount a campaign against him? How does this relate to the image of God as a parent who knows what we need and is 'always more willing to give than we are to ask'?

Perhaps it helps to see this parable as more about justice than about prayer. It seems to be implicit in Jesus' words (v. 7) that prayer is an intimate part of our struggle for justice, and that seeking justice automatically involves prayer.

Our prayer, like our campaigning, must be persistent, not because God is like the unjust judge, but because the world is still full of unjust judges – and we must cry out to God for justice. Our actions and our prayers are inseparable. Both are needed to bring justice for today's widows, orphans and foreigners. And like the persistent widow we need to keep on, and not give up.

> *Lord God, often we give up with our prayers and our campaigns,*
> *because we are unsure, or tired, or just embarrassed.*
> *Give us clear sight to see injustice,*
> *strength to fight it*
> *and perseverance to go on*
> *praying and acting for change.*

Day 9

Loving our enemies
Luke 6:27–36

Be merciful, just as your Father is merciful. (Luke 6:36)

Love your enemies. When I was first introduced to this passage in Sunday School more than thirty years ago, I remember being a little puzzled. I had a loving family, friends and a secure environment – so who were the enemies I was supposed to love? And for many people, thank God, that is still true.

But if by 'enemies' we understand 'people who directly or indirectly cause harm to others', then surely the majority of people in the world today do have enemies. More than half the world's population live on less than £1.20 or € 2 a day. The global economic systems that give us security also contribute to keeping them in poverty.

So how can a family living in poverty 'do good' to the people and systems which are causing their poverty? Jesus' command seems to be over-simplistic, not to say wimpish. Is he asking the poor just to put up with things? Are we all to be submissive doormats?

But perhaps Jesus is not calling for servile submission, but instead for those who are hurt and oppressed to take back the initiative for action. The American theologian Walter Wink points out that, far from inviting his followers to be doormats, Jesus is challenging them to stand up to their enemies. By praying for them, by loving and doing good to them, poor and oppressed people take the initiative and respond to those who are doing them harm.

But this is an even harder thing to ask of someone else than to choose to do for oneself. If we do not feel ourselves to be oppressed, or to have enemies, how can we respond to the needs of those who are and do?

I think the first step is to be willing to be good allies. As allies we can stand beside those who are poor, and make their struggle our struggle. Through organisations like Christian Aid, we can support the fight against global poverty with the gift of our time, money and prayers. And by campaigning for change to some of the economic systems and structures that contribute to global poverty we can help make the voices of the poor be heard.

Lord God, we live in a world of rich and poor,
of oppressors and oppressed.
Help us to stand up with those who are downtrodden,
be their allies and supporters,
and help them to respond to those who do them harm.

Day 10

Specks and planks
Luke 6:37–42

First take the plank out of your eye. (Luke 6:42)

Another Sunday School favourite! And I can remember my confusion because it seemed to me to be far more generous to help someone else with a plank in their eye (though a little strange . . .) before dealing with the speck in one's own!

But of course this is one of Jesus' jokes-with-a-point: be aware of your own faults before pointing out those of others. And most of us are probably very familiar with the sharp tinge of recognition it provokes. Oh how easy it is to remember instances where I have been critical of the 'speck' in my brother or sister's eye while ignoring the 'plank' in my own!

But reading this passage at a personal and spiritual level shouldn't stop us understanding what it also might have to say at a political and economic level. As a guide to international relations it points out the hypocrisy of the powerful countries in the rich world who preach 'do as we say, not as we do' to the countries of the developing world.

In the arena of international trade, poor countries are being denied the right to protect and support their own vulnerable industries and farmers in the way that almost all rich countries have done in the past. But this obvious hypocrisy goes almost completely unchallenged because it's just 'the way of the world'.

Martin Luther King once said that injustice anywhere is a threat to justice everywhere. We can see now more than ever just how interconnected our world is – how a terrorist bombing in one part of the world can provoke war elsewhere. How poverty can lead to the rise of fundamentalism and civil unrest. The double standards that exist on such a massive scale on the international scene surely cannot go on for very much longer.

And to stay hopeful we need to remember that interconnectedness works the other way too. A fairer world, where everyone has the opportunity to earn a decent wage, is also a more secure world for everyone.

We can make a difference in our world. 'Never doubt,' said the American anthropologist Margaret Mead, 'that a small group of thoughtful committed citizens can change the world; indeed, it's the only thing that ever has.'

> *Lord God, we are often overwhelmed when we see the hypocrisy*
> *that takes place on the world stage.*
> *And it's easy to feel powerless in the face of global politics.*
> *Help us to do what we can to work for a fairer, more just*
> *   world,*
> *where all people can live in peace and with hope.*

Day 11

Witnesses to the world
Acts 1:1–9

In a few days you will be baptised with the Holy Spirit.
(Acts 1:5)

Jesus' last words are to commission his disciples to be 'witnesses' to the ends of the earth. Armed with the power of the Holy Spirit, they are to take what they have seen and heard out into the world. They are to begin in the holy city of Jerusalem, and go on to the surrounding territory of Judea, to Samaria and beyond. They are to be the risen Christ's witnesses in the world.

Historically, this passage has been the mandate for church growth and evangelism, and has inspired generations to share their faith with others. In the world today it can inspire us to witness to the good news of God's concern for the poor, the needy and the marginalised.

It seems to me that the institutional churches in the developed world have often lost sight of this truth. They have become mired in the business of maintaining their own position, and in obsessing about the minutiae of doctrine. Preserving historic buildings has all too often taken priority over concern for justice. Defending their own power and privilege has become more important than defending the needs of the poor.

This passage makes clear that the good news of Jesus is not to be limited, but is to be shared throughout the world. The church is to be a missionary organisation – one that sends people out. So the followers of Jesus are to be outward-looking and always on the move, inspired and guided by the Holy Spirit.

Yet churches today often look in at themselves instead, expecting newcomers to conform to 'the way we do things here'. People who are in any way 'different' often feel uncomfortable and unwelcome. Far from being open to people around, they can be cosy clubs for those already inside. So as we endeavour to open our hearts to people around us, this passage is a timely reminder that those people may be a long way away (Samaria), or just the other side of the church wall (Jerusalem).

As an individual it can be hard to stand up for a different way of doing things. But it can happen, and like all human organisations the church is also surely redeemable. This can only come about through the actions of Christians at grass roots – time, perhaps, for a new campaign!

> Lord God, you called the first disciples to be your witnesses in the world.
> Help us to witness to your concern for the poor and the marginalised,
> and to transform your church so that it becomes a beacon in the world,
> reflecting your love to all people.

Day 12

WEEK 2: OPENING OUR HEARTS TO PEOPLE IN NEED

NJONGONKULU NDUNGANE

Giving to those in need
Deuteronomy 14:22–8

Be sure to set aside a tenth of all that your fields produce each year. (Deuteronomy 14:22)

Every year eight million children die of diseases linked to impure water and air pollution; fifty million children are mentally and physically damaged due to poor nutrition; and 130 million children – 80 per cent of them girls – are denied the opportunity to go to school. This is happening in a world in which 20 per cent of the population enjoys 80 per cent of the world's wealth.

In Deuteronomy we encounter God's command to tithe from the richness that he has given us. This is about more than pledging money to a specific or holy cause: it acts out a relationship in which God is primary. It is easy to be indifferent to God, to believe that we do not need the God of mercy in our lives if all is going well and we have position, income and authority. Then, too often, our giving is motivated by some kind of guilt or shame that stems from our wellness or well-being. But if we are like any of the children described above, our attitude to God may rather be one of bitterness, stemming from fear or betrayal.

Our attitude towards giving must come from our deepest sense of relatedness, rather than from obligation or guilt. We are related to one another in the strictest sense because we are created in the image of God. When we reject this human relatedness, we shatter the image of God in us. In Africa the word which describes this understanding of human relationship is *Ubuntu*. It means that 'I cannot be a whole person without you' and 'you cannot be without me'. Laying claim to our relatedness means recognising and upholding relationship. Thus acts of charity become acts that affirm one's own humanity.

In the name of relationship and goodness, we may learn not only to give to those in need, but also to embrace our own neediness, which causes us to live in such excess that it even denies relationship with a future. The God of Abraham, Isaac, Jacob and Jesus calls us out to bring our tithe from the wealth of our lives. Can we really offer anything less?

Eternal God, author and giver of life, you have made us from the dust of the earth and called us into relationship with you and with each other. Grant us the vision to see our relatedness as a reflection of your love, and to offer our lives and our gifts as a means of ordering our lives. Amen.

Day 13

The gift of freedom
Deuteronomy 15:12–18

In the seventh year you must let [your servant] go free. And when you release him, do not send him away empty-handed. (Deuteronomy 15:12b–13)

When South Africa emerged from the fires of the struggle to end apartheid, it did so with what appeared to be a miraculous transformation from an oppressive political system to a democratic one representing all people. However, poverty and inequality, the legacy of a past of economic and social distress and dysfunction, remain the major challenges before our nation today.

You see, freedom is not free. As we struggle with supplying adequate water, reasonable housing, redistribution of land and the effects of HIV and AIDS in our communities, we are still paying the price for the past. Freedom is not free. It costs all of us.

We did not heed the biblical injunction to send forth the recently freed with something in their hands. Not many nations which have gone through such dramatic changes in their political and economic order as South Africa have been able to provide for the people. The tragic effect is grotesque injustice and poverty that is sometimes worse than in the dark days of oppression.

Striving for wholeness, inclusiveness, fairness, equity and respect for the other person is what our mission is to be. But where you live today is no different. We all have dreams of freedom. But freedom isn't free. Perhaps it would be good in this season of preparation to look about us and discover again where freedom is denied or withheld. To face again the harsh reality of the crucifixion of Christ is to be reminded of the brokenness all around us. It is also to learn again of hope. Because we know that God raised Jesus from the dead. Thus our age is the age of hope and we are agents of hope, knowing what, with God's help, we can do.

Almighty God, in Jesus you said, 'Behold, I make all things new.' Help us to make those things new that have destroyed the lives of our brothers and sisters. Help us to end discrimination, neglect and violence. Give us the will to end poverty and injustice, and bring equality and hope to all people. Let us make all things new with you. Amen.

Day 14

Cities of refuge
Deuteronomy 19:1–7

Set aside for yourselves three cities. (Deuteronomy 19:2)

At the end of each day, I find myself seeking the refuge of my garden in Bishopscourt. In this place I can regain a sense of perspective and peace in what is otherwise a wearying and often emotionally crushing place of work. This need for refuge was known even to the earliest days of our forebears in Israel. As they were conquering the land, they were warned to establish 'cities of refuge' to harbour those accused of crimes against humanity. I have often wondered why, but on reflection have come to see that even a prison can be a refuge.

Robben Island, that infamous place of deprivation and terror in the old apartheid South Africa, has been transformed into a world centre of peace and reconciliation. The potent symbolism of this place is not one of reputation only, but incarnate in the fact that from this island came one who could lead South Africa into trans-formation – Nelson Mandela. The island has a positive influence upon all who travel to its shores or know its reputation. It is part of the spirit of hope, that reconciling effect that people who were incarcerated on the island can bring to the world. I know this personally, for I was one of them.

Places of refuge are needed in all of our communities. They bring to people the capacity to allow change to happen and to create space for re-visioning the world. We are in need of more such places in an increasingly small global community. Have we provided for space to breathe clean air, or smell the fragrance of flowers on a midsummer's evening? Have we allowed for there to be places where persecutors and prosecutors do not go, save for refuge?

For people of faith, there is one refuge which cannot be overlooked or ignored. That is Jesus. With him, we have slowly but surely come to accept that his love for us is unconditional and lasts for ever. Like no other person in our lives, he accepts us even when we cannot accept ourselves. Have we accepted his invitation to the refuge he offers?

> *Lord Jesus Christ, we flee to you in times of trouble and despair. But make us mindful that we can take refuge in your love and there enjoy your special peace. Grant us gentleness of spirit, openness of mind and willingness of heart to come to you. Amen.*

Day 15

Feeding the crowds
Luke 9:10–17

Jesus replied, 'You give them something to eat' . . . Taking the
five loaves and the two fish . . . he gave thanks and broke
them. Then he gave them to the disciples to set before the
people. They all ate and were satisfied.
(Luke 9:13a, 16–17a)

Too often the news of the day is filled with overt signs of violence and human cruelty. But to me there is no image more shocking and more violent than one of children scavenging for food in a dump, which, tragically, is a common scene in the developing world. Knowing that we all have a mandate from our Lord to 'feed the hungry and clothe the naked' should shape our commitment and inform our vocations. Often it is understood as no more than rhetoric.

I have dedicated myself to the principle that the developed world, out of the implicit relatedness of being human, has a moral responsibility to forgive the indebtedness of the developing world. Why, you might ask? Because much of this debt was organised under corrupt and deceitful regimes; much of this debt has long since been repaid, only the interest remains. And it is those interest payments that take the food from the mouths of our children.

But there is more. I have redoubled my efforts to work for economic systems which put people first and profits second, and for systems based on respect for the environment. And finally I am working for democratic accountability and transparency. All of this and more is what I am about in the new South Africa. But our Lord's command to 'feed them' remains.

We cannot turn the clock back to a pre-colonial period, so we must ask our families in the North, who have long enjoyed the benefits of our work and our resources, to support these transitions. You have the ability to think and act. You have the ability to influence authority and persuade those in power. You also command resources and investments. Think of us and think of Jesus, who said, 'Feed them'.

Author of Life, we come to you in repentance for the sins and abuses of the past, and beg your forgiveness for the destruction of communities and cultures and environments. Enable us to reach through our inertia and fear to feed your people wherever they are. Give us courage in the face of political pressure. Grant us the wisdom to use our resources to your will and to your glory. Give us the spirit of Jesus. Amen.

Day 16

Who is my neighbour?
Luke 10:25–37

'Teacher . . . what must I do to inherit eternal life?' . . .
'Go and do likewise.' (Luke 10:25, 37)

We live in a world often described as a global village. We all know that events in one country or even one community can have tragic consequences all over the world. Need we look beyond the recent wars in Iraq and Afghanistan and even in Africa? Perhaps this is a necessary step for human beings to come to a deeper understanding of our interdependence upon one another and our mutual entanglements. Nothing has made this more personal and yet more global than the rapid spread of HIV around the world and the pandemic of AIDS.

At the heart of our response to HIV and AIDS I have had to travel the road with those who are infected. I have become one of the affected through the experience. Recently, a group of HIV+ young persons asked me, 'Does anyone care? Does anyone care if we live or die? Does anyone really care?' It is the same question that the man going from Jerusalem to Jericho, beset by robbers, must have asked himself and those who passed by.

We begin any response by extending our hearts and hands in love. But we must be careful not to further stigmatise those who suffer. Because people of faith have long associated sickness with sin, it is indeed difficult to break our pattern of judgment about cause and effect. We cannot stand in judgment of anyone living with or dying from the effects of HIV and AIDS any more than we can blame the man on the road from Jerusalem to Jericho for being in the way of robbers and thieves. AIDS is a disease caused by a virus, not a sin, or, as our church has proclaimed, 'AIDS is not a judgment from God.'

It may be helpful to move beyond judgment to compassion; to leave our attitudes of blame and guilt behind on the road, as we move towards deeper commitment to those who suffer all around us. We need not look for the victims of robbery and theft: we need only look out of our door and there we will find the need. Jesus reminds us that establishing this relationship with the suffering and wounded will somehow cause us to experience eternal life. Maybe we should just try it.

Lord God, Lamb of God, who suffers and is broken: grant us to reach beyond our fear and guilt, fill us with courage and trust, engage us in the work of reclaiming your world that we might with them know life which is eternal. Amen.

Day 17

Not silver or gold
Acts 3:1–10

Silver or gold I do not have, but what I have I give you.
(Acts 3:6)

We are all servants of God. For too long it has been easy to categorise one group of people, namely the clergy, as the servants of God. But if we look carefully to the Bible we discover that while Jesus is our model for servanthood, he never expected that it would be his alone. In fact, on the night before he died, he gathered with his followers, and washed their feet before supper. He reminded them that he was their friend and that they must do as much for each other.

It is a searing moment in our lives when we realise that we have all the gifts necessary to be faithful servants of Jesus. Jesus does not glorify subservience, he ennobles the free choice to serve. Throughout my province in southern Africa, we too see such service rendered daily by the many voluntary carers to those living with or dying from HIV/AIDS. We see them making the choice to serve, to give what they have of themselves.

We also know of many grandmothers who, late in life, have taken on more children orphaned by disease, poverty and violence. Acts of faith and acts of courage are the daily fare of our people. While we are enabled to do a great deal, we look for partners of hope. We know that the daily press of life in the North is not as difficult as it is in the global South. We know that in the resource-rich parts of the world, the tools for caring may be in abundance, whereas where I live much is lacking.

As Jesus sought to undo the power of subservience, to break the pattern of domination of one group of people over another, he modelled true freedom in giving his power away and offering a service of love. Out of this experience, he is giving all that he has and invites us to do the same. The Christian message is radical in that it addresses and challenges all models of power and domination. And the way it addresses them is to invite us all to give away our power in the service of love. Thus, the issue of our relatedness lies at the heart of Jesus' perpetual question to us, 'Do you love me?'

Gracious God, you invite us into relationship that we may be emboldened to give up our power in the service of love. While our hearts may be hardened, and our spirits shrivelled, let us receive what you have for us, that we may be healed and made whole, in Jesus Christ our Lord. Amen.

Day 18

A special ministry
Acts 6:1–7

Brothers and sisters, choose seven men from among you who are known to be full of the Spirit and wisdom. We will turn this responsibility over to them. (Acts 6:3, NIV Inclusive)

The experience of women in Africa, built as it is on patriarchal cultures and traditions, provides the opportunity to re-evaluate some of the classical understandings of the Christ. The experience of many women is one of struggle – struggle against poverty, disease, oppression, war and death itself. The Christ whom African women know, however, is the one who is friend, healer, consoler, liberator and companion. It is clear that Christ affirms the goodness of women, helps them bear life's burdens and sorrows, and challenges those who oppress them.

Because Jesus enters this world and challenges the dominant structures of power and transforms that challenge by self-giving love, there can be no tolerance for oppressive and exclusive structures which cause another human being to be lessened.

Because the church was founded in the midst of empire and conquest, the issues of power – who has it, who wants it and who earns it – have often been ignored or denied in our Christian history. There are times when we Christians seem to be embarrassed about even discussing or admitting our power. We are not free if we feel or experience ourselves to be powerless. And we can only give away power that we possess. Jesus demonstrated that much in his welcome of the outcasts and the broken, and in his eating with sinners and women!

Because it is clear that we are not called to maintain the status quo but rather to learn from our experience, we know that as human beings we find our own humanity only in relationship to others – *Ubuntu*. Since this is the essence of our experience, then the experience of women and their faith calls us to acknowledge and uphold them for the special calling that God demands. Only by breaking through the tortured and traumatic cultural and social histories of both the North and the South are we able to move on this journey towards wholeness and renewal. And when we arrive, we will find women and men together as equal partners in our salvation.

Come, Holy Spirit, and fill us with your wisdom. Help us to break down the doors and traditions which have separated us. Help us to see that we cannot rest until all of us are free: male and female, rich and poor, sick and well, young and old. And grant us love and acceptance for those who have been too long held apart in the name of your church. Amen.

Day 19

WEEK THREE: OPENING OUR HEARTS TO PEOPLE OF FAITH

CHRIS SUGDEN

God's obedient people
Deuteronomy 5:22–33

So that it might go well with them and their children for ever. (Deuteronomy 5:29)

Moses knows he will never see the land of promise. He desperately wants it to go well for the people in the land he cannot enter. All he can do, and the best he can do, is to entrust to his people what God said to him. The people go into the land with no Moses to lead them. But they will have the laws and decrees of God.

Both Moses and the people had learnt through spectacular experiences on Mount Sinai that not only could a man live if God speaks with him, but a man can live because God speaks with him. God's words bring and ensure life – 'that it might go well with them and their children for ever'.

God's laws and decrees enshrine respect for human life, human relationships and human achievement: no murder, no adultery, no stealing and no coveting. Such conclusions are based not on focus groups or surveys, but on faith that we are accountable to our creator. Faith is seeing that this is the way things should be. Relationships built on faith are accountable to God.

Tony Blair spoke of this during the war in Iraq. In May 2003 Peter Stothard, editor of *The Times*, wrote: 'He speaks of being ready to "meet my Maker" and answer for "those who have died or have been horribly maimed as a result of my decision". He accepts that others who share belief in his Maker, who believe in "the same God" assess that the Last Judgment will be against him.' Stothard concludes, however, 'If I am asked whether the Prime Minister, as well as feeling the political risk of war, feels powerfully and personally its worst individual results, I will say that he does.'

As the second Moses, Jesus leads his people out of the land of slavery to sin into the promised land of freedom to do the will of God from the heart. His laws and decrees enshrine further that religion is a matter not of birth or race, but of choice; that obedience is from the heart. As Madonna put it, 'If we truly believed that every act of denigrating somebody is a small form of murder – the negative energy you create by talking badly – we'd never do it again.'

Our readings this week explore relationships built on faith.

> O God of Moses, our Father in faith, help us listen to and obey what you told Moses. Give us the trust that your words bring life; help us see how it might go well with us and our children when our relationships are built on faith in obedience to your commands.

Day 20

Accepting one another
Luke 5:27–32

*A large crowd of tax collectors and others were
eating with them. (Luke 5:29)*

Relationships built on faith believe people can change.

What did Jesus see in Levi? He saw more than a tax collector. He saw beyond the greed and treachery of those who bought from the Roman occupation forces the right to levy the taxes they demanded from their own people. He saw beyond the hatred of fellow Jews for someone who profited from the Gentile occupation of God's own land. He saw someone whose gifts of memory, writing and attention to detail, so twisted in the service of greed, would be liberated by his gospel of the kingdom. Levi would be freed from slavery to the unforgiving demands of mammon for one lifetime to sharing life through his words with a hundred generations.

Jesus saw in Levi someone who could change. Jesus excludes no one from his invitation. He is not anti-rich. Neither do poor Christians have to stand powerless before rich people. They have in the gospel something to enrich even the lives of those who have everything, and to give them good reason for a party.

Levi rejoiced publicly over what Jesus had brought into his life. Such a celebration attracted party poopers whose sense of what was fitting was gravely offended. The Pharisees were not priests. But they believed that if all the people of God, not only the priests, kept all the law of God for one day, then the kingdom of God would come and the Holy Land would be freed of the Gentile oppressor.

So they only accepted hospitality from one another. Jesus' behaviour, in accepting the hospitality of those who contaminated Jewish purity, broke the strict details of the law and would destroy religion as the Pharisees knew it.

Jesus' inclusiveness does not condone sin. He describes the world as a hospital – sick people are not excluded but welcomed for a process of repentance, change, restoration and healing.

What do we see in people who are not like us? Are they people to be spurned? Or do we welcome them to the hospital in which we are the in-patients? Do we give thanks that we are not like others or do we see others as people to be welcomed and invited to meet Jesus who will change and claim all their lives – that it will go well with them and their children for ever?

> *Lord, bring to our minds those who in our worse moments we are glad have no part in our lives and are not in our circle. Help us see them with your eyes by seeing ourselves first, that we all live in a hospital where your healing is available to all, even to them, and may they be healed as well.*

Day 21

The faith of a foreigner
Luke 7:1–10

I have not found such great faith even in Israel. (Luke 7:9)

Relationships built on faith believe that Jesus can and will help. Respeck! The centurion was a man under authority. His orders carried not his own authority, but the authority of the Roman emperor. That is why one hundred soldiers obeyed him. Having authority meant that he could expect obedience precisely because he was accountable to a higher authority.

The centurion was also a man who had won and deserved respect in his own right. He represented the Roman occupying power, but trod lightly in another's homeland. The colonised themselves recognised him as one who loved their nation. They publicly gave him the credit for building a meeting place for a religion not his own. And he valued his servants.

The Jews had good reason to hate this representative of Roman power which brooked no opposition, which had murdered hundreds of their countrymen over many decades of occupation. Yet this centurion's Jewish subjects pleaded his obvious merit. And even more strangely, the centurion urged that he was not worthy to have this Jewish rabbi trouble himself to come to his house.

He saw Jesus' authority and power clearly enough to ask him only for a word. Yet Jesus gave no word. All Jesus did was to add to the praise the centurion had already received – contrasting his faith favourably with that of God's own people. For the centurion had seen what God's own people had not: that Jesus had God's authority, that his word was to be obeyed as God's word and had the power to bring life. Though an outstanding man in his community, he still came to Jesus.

Jesus had seen what the Jews had not: someone who belonged among God's people, not by birth, nor even by the outstanding behaviour which commended him to his conquered subjects, but by seeing in Jesus one with the power and authority of God.

Jesus includes those like Levi who recognise they are in hospital and need a doctor, and the centurion who sees and recognises Jesus for who he is – the one who has the power, authority and willingness of God to help and heal. Jesus includes people, not on any terms, but those who repent and recognise in him one who has the words and does the work of God.

> *Lord, bring to our minds those whose power we have reason to hate or despise. Help us see that among them may be those who put us to shame in their love for and trust in you. Help us, like the Jewish elders, to be willing to introduce them and their concerns to you.*

Day 22

God's forgiven people
Luke 7:36–50

Her many sins have been forgiven — for she loved much.
(Luke 7:47)

Relationships built on faith believe we are forgiven and being restored.

Behaviour proves who people really are. To Simon the Pharisee Jesus' behaviour in allowing himself to be touched by this prostitute showed conclusively that he was not a prophet. Otherwise he would have seen this woman for who she was — a person who shared her love and her body without any concern for social propriety, for the sanctity of the family, or for the laws of Israel and of God. Simon almost patronisingly forgave Jesus because of his ignorance.

Jesus could see what Simon was thinking — the mind's construction written in the face. He tells Simon a parable. A parable invites the listener to make a judgment about a particular situation.

The classic parable was told when Nathan rebuked King David for marrying Bathsheba and having her husband killed. To rebuke a king is not easy. So Nathan asked David to judge about a rich man who welcomed a guest not with a lamb slain from his own large flocks, but with the only lamb belonging to his neighbour. David gave a magisterial response — the man who did this should die. Nathan had only to say 'You are the man' (2 Samuel 12:7). David had nowhere to hide.

In this case Jesus asked Simon to judge which of two debtors would owe a greater debt of gratitude to a moneylender and thus love him the more. Simon gives the obvious answer: the one who had the bigger debt of 500 days' wages cancelled. In making his judgment Simon has judged himself, as all hearers of parables do.

Simon's minimal hospitality to Jesus proved that he was in no great debt to Jesus. Perhaps he thought he was doing Jesus a favour in inviting him to dinner and that Jesus was in debt to him. The woman's extravagant gestures of anointing Jesus' feet with perfume, weeping and wiping her tears away with her tresses, proved she loved Jesus dearly and was in great debt to him.

Relationships built on faith see in Jesus the one who has forgiven us a debt we can never manage to pay.

Lord, please prevent us from ever thinking that you are in our debt, or that our love for you can ever adequately express our gratitude for forgiving the debt of our sins.

Day 23

Sharing in the kingdom
Luke 12:22–34

*Do not be afraid . . . for your Father has been pleased
to give you the kingdom. (Luke 12:32)*

Relationships built on faith deal with insecurity.

The opposite of faith is not unbelief but anxiety. How then does faith deal with anxiety? Anxiety comes from believing that your identity and security are based on what you possess. In the preceding parable in Luke 12, of the man who built bigger barns, Jesus shows the problem that is inherent in believing that all one's goods are one's own and not held in stewardship for the Owner. There is no end to the resources needed to fill the hole created by trying to find identity in replacing the Owner with what one owns. So there is nothing to spare for the needs of the poor.

The solution to the problem is to see that God feeds the birds, clothes the flowers and knows that his children need food and clothes. The Father asks that his children have their priorities right – to seek first the Father's kingdom – and they will find that he will meet their expenses. The Father delights to give his children the kingdom. They will also find that they become like their Father in adopting his priorities and reflecting his care. They will in their turn feed, clothe and know and give to those who are poor.

They will have treasure in heaven – treasure in heaven is precisely reproducing God's love in providing for the poor. Paul says so also in 1 Timothy 6:18–19: 'Command [those who are rich in this present world] to do good, to be rich in good deeds, and to be generous and willing to share. In this way they will lay up treasure for themselves as a firm foundation for the coming age, so that they may take hold of the life that is truly life.'

Relationships built on faith include providing for the needs of the poor. Those with faith believe that God will provide both for their needs and for the needs of the poor, often through them themselves. If we do not believe that God will meet our needs, then we are not free to meet the needs of the poor. Instead it takes all our resources to solve the problems of our identities and anxieties on our own. And this no one has ever succeeded in doing.

Lord, as we pray for the needs of the poor to be met, help us to see with the eyes of faith that in meeting their needs we also will be meeting our own deep needs for security and identity, as we learn to trust you for your provision as our heavenly Father.

Day 24

Christian fellowship
Acts 2:42–7

*They broke bread in their homes and ate together
with glad and sincere hearts. (Acts 2:46)*

Relationships built on faith use the resources that the people of faith already have to build community, not resources they don't have.

What counts as a church, a community of Christian believers? Is it what a bishop or a committee recognises as a church? It may be, but only if it follows the biblical example of a Christian community that follows the lead of Jesus. If it does, then anyone can build a Christian community.

Acts 2:42 sets out four hallmarks of a Christian community. It's a teaching community: the apostles' teaching is taught as the truth, and innovations or fresh knowledge do not supersede the authority of the Scriptures. Then the community is a fellowship, where people value their relationships as brothers and sisters in the Christian family, and find and give support and encouragement to one another in the faith. It's not a gathering that people seek to escape as quickly as possible after worship because religion is a private affair.

This community is eucharistic: people break bread regularly in remembrance of the death of Jesus for their sins. And finally, and most importantly, it's a praying community. People pray and depend on the intervention of God in their lives and in the life of the world; they don't use prayer to sanctify their own left- or right-wing ideology. They expect God to intervene, especially, as Jesus did, for the benefit of the poor. So the earliest Christians worshipped God together, even in an institution that was under God's judgment (the temple would be destroyed within forty years). And they also worshipped God in their homes, through giving thanks at meals, family prayers and prayer with others as they met. For them religion was not something to be kept in church.

Today a Christian community on this model will be recognised in wider society as making a significant and welcome contribution to the well-being of the wider community, not ignored as being only a group of people who are simply concerned with themselves. To such a community God can entrust newborn babes in the faith, for they will be nurtured and built up in a healthy Christian life.

Lord, please make our Christian community healthy enough to entrust to us those whom you are bringing to new birth in the faith.

Day 25

The scattered church
Acts 11:19–30

*When [Barnabas] arrived and saw the evidence
of the grace of God, he was glad. (Acts 11:23)*

Relationships built on faith encourage new life in others.

The Christian faith was spreading through the Jewish communities, despite strong persecution. But since this was God's work and not limited by the men and women who carried it out, the bounds of race and culture were not respected. Gentiles came to faith in Antioch.

This would cause trouble in the church. Later Peter and Paul would publicly disagree on how members of these two hostile communities could bury their differences in one Christian community. Peter's initial answer was separate development. Paul stood for expanding the very idea of what the Christian community was to be: where people from different races, tribes and languages would be in one fellowship together because at the cross Jesus had broken down the barriers between races and cultures. All served one Lord and had received one Spirit. Faith in Jesus was inclusive of all peoples.

How was the mother church in Jerusalem to deal with this unforeseen development? They sent Barnabas to check matters out. When he saw something new that was evidence of the grace of God, he rejoiced. He saw that the Lord was at work and in control and urged the new believers only to remain true to him.

When we see something new, do we look for evidence of the grace of God? Are we glad, judgmental or jealous? Do we look for evidence that God is in control, or think that the show should be ours?

Barnabas brought in resources to help. Given the need to include Jews and Gentiles in the Christian community, the choice of Saul, who came from a strict Jewish background, was inspired and witnessed to the transformation in all concerned. Barnabas saw God's work not only in the Gentile Christians in Antioch but also in the newly converted Saul. He encouraged them all. When we hear of someone new, do we bring them in and make them welcome and give them the opportunity to use their gifts in the Lord's household?

Then they heard the prophecy of a famine, and responded by making provision for their brothers in Judea. The new Gentile believers had clearly been taught their responsibilities across the cultural divide to those in need in the Jewish communities.

Lord, help us remember that the work is yours and that you will provide the resources in people and materials to build your people as instruments of your work and love, often in surprising ways that expand our vision. Give us hearts that seek to encourage and support others in your work.

WEEK 4: OPENING OUR HEARTS TO FAMILY

WENDY BRAY

Mothers together
Luke 1:39–45

Blessed is she who has believed that what the Lord has said to her will be accomplished! (Luke 1:45)

Here is a scene familiar throughout history. Two expectant mothers greeting each other, sharing the excitement of their pregnancies and dreaming dreams together. It is a scene so easy to imagine. Yet Mary and Elizabeth were two very special 'expectant' mothers; their expectancy was shared by a wider world. All creation was waiting for these two babies, the first to herald the coming of the second. Two extraordinary births followed by extraordinary lives.

Luke's very human account of the meeting of Mary and Elizabeth reveals just a hint of their breathless, bewildered comprehension, of the uniqueness of their friendship, and the awesome privilege of God's calling on their lives. Did they also dare to anticipate the pain and anguish that awaited them in years to come as God their saviour worked out his plan? Mary certainly recognises in the song of praise that follows that salvation has *already come* with the presence of each child in the womb. She must have known, too, that both she and Elizabeth had been called to mother 'against the odds': that alongside the joy there would be pain; alongside nurture, loss.

The world over, mothers still mother against the odds. They wave photographs of 'lost' sons in front of TV cameras and keep vigil in sparsely equipped hospitals alongside war-wounded children. We watch helplessly as a malnourished mother struggles to breast-feed her dying baby, her grip on hope as desperate as her child's on her empty breast. This is indeed mothering against the odds. It is daring to go on believing in the impossible, hoping against hope, loving beyond belief because of the calling of motherhood.

Mary must often have recalled the words the angel Gabriel had given her, as she struggled to keep an eternal perspective on the pain of her son's journey to the cross. But could she have begun to understand how God would turn the world upside down through the salvation given by the life, death and resurrection of her son?

Yet Mary believed that what the Lord had said to her would be accomplished. 'I am the Lord's servant,' she declared, and with those words she surrendered her parenting into the hands of the God she trusted, and was blessed. Mothers – and fathers – among us will all too often be called to do the same.

> *Father God,*
> *Turn our hearts and minds to those who mother 'against the odds' across our broken world.*
> *Help us to uphold motherhood as part of your mission and, as we do so, to trust you for our children and believe in our hearts that 'nothing is impossible with God'.*

Day 27

God and the family
Deuteronomy 6:1–9

Impress [these words] on your children. Talk about them when you sit at home and when you walk along the road, when you lie down and when you get up. (Deuteronomy 6:7)

These beautiful verses emphasise something of God the Father's interest in the lives of his children and his intimate concern for the practicality of his word as the basis for family life.

Our children are bombarded by conflicting messages. 'Choose this!' they are implored, 'Follow that!'– messages which reach into the very heart of our home and family life via the media, merchandising and peer pressure. But here God gives us clear guidelines to help us counteract those influences, guidelines which are relevant even in our contemporary world of conflicting messages and broken promises.

These verses draw attention to the centrality of loving God in all we do and of reminding our children of God's blueprint for living on a daily basis. We are not to compartmentalise our family life into 'the God bit' on Sunday, 'the school/work bit' during the week and 'the sport bit' on a Saturday, but to daily eat, speak, read and write the love and law of God in everything we do.

There is a clear and practical challenge here, to which we might respond.

Where do we see God's word written around our homes? How often do we bring it into everyday family conversation? Perhaps the nearest we have come to 'tying them as symbols on our hands' has been through the use of 'What Would Jesus Do?' wristbands, colourful mnemonic strips reminding us to involve Jesus in our daily decision-making.

But are there ways in which we can take God's words to heart – by 'writing them on the door frames of our houses and gates'? Above our stairs we have hung a cross-stitch sampler which I sewed when we first moved into our home. It contains words from the book of Joshua: 'As for me and my house, we will serve the Lord' (Joshua 24:15). It is a daily reminder that our family is endeavouring to love and live for, with, and because of the unfathomable love of God, who calls us to love him 'with all our soul and strength'.

God's message of love and salvation is a universal one which needs to be heard more than ever before across a love-starved world. Let's not just write it on our gateposts. Let's find ways on this pathway to Easter to shout it from our rooftops too!

> *God, whose very word is life,*
> *may your laws and love be ever on our lips:*
> *spoken at the bedsides of our children,*
> *celebrated at the heart of our home,*
> *illustrated in the covenant of our marriages,*
> *kept in the promise of our friendships,*
> *shared alongside the tears of our neighbours,*
> *and taken by us into all the world.*

Day 28

Jesus and the children
Luke 18:15–17

Jesus called the little children to him and said, 'Let the little children come to me, and do not hinder them, for the kingdom of God belongs to such as these.' (Luke 18:16)

As Jesus begins his final journey to his royal capital, Jerusalem, Luke recounts the King's teaching about the nature of his kingdom. It's teaching which is begun in the midst of and illustrated by those to whom he gives high kingdom status: children.

There is a well-known illustration which has hung on Sunday School walls for generations. You might remember it as part of your own Christian heritage. It shows Jesus standing on a hill looking down at the faces of a crowd of seemingly quiet and well-behaved children of every nationality. It's a much-loved image, but a somewhat unrealistic one. Jesus, we feel sure, would be down at the children's level, or lifting them to his. He would have known the importance of eye contact with little ones, would have been laughing at their antics, joining in their rough-and-tumble games and answering their eager questions. He would know just how to encourage the timid and still the fractious, and would gently but firmly placate them in their squabbles.

Jesus gave children respect and understanding; he was moved to heal them often and involved them in his teaching and ministry. It was a small boy's packed lunch that he used to feed a crowd of thousands, and on this occasion it is a childlike attitude of trust and acceptance that he uses to illustrate the right way to receive the kingdom of God, and to live within it. More than that, I think

Jesus just enjoyed the company of children and delighted in the way they enjoyed his. It's a similar relationship of sincerity, dependence, mutual delight and trust that he calls us into as heirs of his kingdom.

Jesus rebuked the disciples when they tried to prevent children and babies from coming to him. How easy it is for us to inadvertently do so ourselves – to mistakenly believe that our church-based children's work is little more than a baby-sitting service or an 'out of school' club. Whenever I hear the name of the children's evangelism team Children Worldwide, I am immediately reminded of the huge burden of responsibility we still have to bring children of every nationality, lifestyle, family background and age to the arms of Jesus, 'for the kingdom of God belongs to such as these'. And it is through children that we adults can learn something vital of how to live within it.

> *Like a child of the King*
> *let me know your kingdom.*
> *Like a child taught at your feet*
> *let me hear your word.*
> *Like a child held to your breast*
> *let me know your love.*
> *That I may live in the King's presence,*
> *run in his courts of praise*
> *and invite others in.*

Day 29

Friends and family
Luke 4:38–44

So he bent over her and rebuked the fever, and it left her.
She got up at once and began to wait on them. (Luke 4:39)

Jesus was probably getting to know Simon's mother-in-law well. Perhaps she often prepared meals for him and his followers, and Simon's home, which she shared, was one of the homes where Jesus was always shown warm hospitality and could rest and relax at the end of a busy day. On this day, Simon's mother-in-law became one of the 'many' whom Jesus healed. 'She got up at once', we are told, 'and began to wait on them.' I know my mother-in-law would do the same!

Sustained by her provision, Jesus continues to heal the sick and cast out demons in the wider community throughout the rest of the evening. Yet while his healing ministry liberated many, we must notice that Jesus gave priority to his teaching about the kingdom of God. The next day he turns away from the crowds: 'I must preach the good news of the kingdom of God to the other towns also, because that is why I was sent' (v. 43).

For Jesus, spiritual health and wholeness come before physical health and healing. We can learn much about healing and wholeness from these verses. God does heal, and heal miraculously, today. But ultimately he is more concerned with the state of our hearts than the state of our health. Often he will delay healing, as Jesus did so often in these Gospel accounts, because there is work to be done 'on the way'. Or he will leave healing aside to accomplish greater and better things, perhaps not in 'other towns', but in other ways – both for the one who is sick and for God's kingdom.

Now, as on earth, Jesus is intimately concerned with the lives of our family and our friends. He hears us when we bring their weakness and sickness before him. He will weep with us often, sustain us as we minister to them, and respond with compassion and care. Sometimes he will bring healing. But we would do well to listen to what else he may have to say. For he will always respond to us in the knowledge of the wider purposes of God, which may, as yet, be hidden from us.

We may need to learn to trust what we cannot see, that one day we may know wonders that for now we cannot comprehend.

As we bring our family, our community, our world before you
for healing, remind us that you see the wider picture that
your plan projects.
You have written the screenplay.
You have set the plot.
And while we only see your story frame by frame, you know its
beginning and its end.
Help us to trust you until the grand finale.

Day 30

A father's love
Luke 8:40–42a and 49–56

Then a man named Jairus, a ruler of the synagogue, came and fell at Jesus' feet, pleading with him to come to his house because his only daughter, a girl of about twelve, was dying. (Luke 8:41–2)

'My little girl is dying.' It is an impassioned plea from a father's heart. Jairus' faith fills Jesus with compassion and they set off to the family home together amidst a pressing crowd.

But again, there is work to be done 'on the way'. Jesus won't be hurried and is apparently delayed by the needs of others. It's easy to imagine poor Jairus hopping from one foot to the other with impatience as Jesus speaks to the sick woman who has broken into his journey with her own desperate needs. Then a messenger arrives and all appears lost. The 'little girl' is dead. We can almost hear the collective groan of the crowd, and see Jairus drop his face into his hands. But Jesus is in control. 'Just believe', he says.

Once again there were bigger issues to deal with. This is a time of teaching about faith in action, not just for Jairus but for the disciples alongside Jesus. He wants to teach them how to face life-and-death situations in assurance of his control, simply because he is with them. If they are to fulfil his purpose in mission they will need to understand that it is only when they are 'with Jesus' in a deeper sense that they will be able to meet the needs of others. There is a lesson there for us too. Then, with the simple act of taking the hand of a young girl, Jesus demonstrates the deeper assurance they could have. That he is indeed in control of past, present and future. Sickness and health, life and death. How wonderful to have Jesus 'take your hand' and lead you into life!

I recently listened to a young woman working in southern Africa with children whose lives have been devastated by HIV/AIDS. She said that it would be easy to become overwhelmed by the extent of the HIV epidemic, but that she daily reminds herself that each time she takes the hand of a child she is doing it with the love and compassion of Jesus. That he sees each upturned face, knows each broken life intimately, and as she takes a hand, he takes it too.

Jesus still has the power to take the hands of his children and lead them from death into life.

As I stretch out my hand into the lives of others
  let me do so in your name.
Remind me of your healing hand:
the hand that touches, brings peace, and leads us into life;
the hand with which we are upheld, protected, and given
   direction;
the hand upon which our names are engraved for eternity,
  because of a Father's love.

Day 31

Two sons
Luke 15:13–31

While he was still a long way off, his father saw him and was filled with compassion for him; he ran to his son, threw his arms around him and kissed him. (Luke 15:20)

It's the ultimate tale of what writer and speaker Jeff Lucas calls 'outrageous grace' – grace that is so amazing that it is almost unbelievable. This is the reconciliation story that with Hollywood treatment would break box office records and win Oscars.

The son who has turned his back on his father's love and provision has squandered all he has been given and, recognising the error of his ways, knows there is nowhere else to go except back to the father who loves him. Even then, he assumes he will face servitude rather than sonship. Yet the father loves his son, and not only looks out for him but runs towards him, arms open wide, and welcomes him back with honour and celebration.

We sometimes need to be reminded that the parable Jesus told is about *two* sons: the son welcomed back to his father's house, and the one who had remained, working away at his father's business. It is also as much a story about the prodigals who leave and then return to our *churches* as it is about our return to God the Father.

Those of us who have never left but remained faithful may resent the Father's welcome of those who walked away because of liturgy or lifestyle. But what might we, the elder brothers in this context, have contributed to make them leave in the first place? What petty rule or regulation did we place above their spiritual growth and security? Perhaps we objected to the colour of their hair, the style of their worship, the demands they made on our time, or their way of life.

But God's grace is for every prodigal, including our long-lost brothers and sisters in Christ. We may carry on working, but the Father never stops his daily vigil, his walk to a spot on the road where he can see a few miles beyond. And from there he will strain his eyes into the distance, looking out for those sons he has lost. Ought we not to join him at the bend of the road occasionally?

And when we are not at that bend of the road, let's be challenged to get our house in order so we can welcome the homecomers, as the Father has welcomed us. And then we can join the party too.

Never let me forget your open arms, Father.
When I was still far off you met me with your 'outrageous grace'.
You gave me a homecoming I will never forget.
So take me to the bend of the road with you,
so that I can look out for my wayward brothers and sisters
and bring them home.

Day 32

The wider family
Luke 8:19–21

*My mother and brothers are those who hear God's word
and put it into practice. (Luke 8:21)*

Jesus' family have come to the rescue. He was facing burnout as
far as they were concerned, and was undoubtedly making them
the source of more than a little local gossip. His brothers, who
probably didn't believe a word of his claims at this time, are here
with their mother Mary, to get him to see sense. And Mary, only
half understanding the extraordinary life of her first son, has heard
their appeal: 'He'll listen to you! You're his mother!' Yet when they
arrive, they are unable to reach him and have to wait outside.

Jesus wasn't being insensitive to Mary's concern for him or
rejecting his family's care. And although we aren't told whether they
met, it is unlikely that he would have ignored them. But in the
context of his teaching, it was important to make the point – to the
crowd as well as to his family – that his relationships with those
who believe in him have at least equal claim on him. Jesus' family is
all-inclusive: this is his message both to those who are related to
him and also to us, who, in the spiritual sense, have been adopted
by his Father and brought into the family.

It's not always easy to apply Jesus' family policy even to the
Christians in our local church! But we *are* family. For some we may
be the *only* family, which may challenge us to open our homes as
well as our hearts. And we have 'family' across the world in faith
situations vastly different from our own, for whom we also have a
responsibility. For many, following Jesus is not the soft option it is

for us. They suffer loss of livelihood, imprisonment, torture and death, because they refuse to stop living and sharing the gospel. In 1999 a staggering 164,000 of our Christian family worldwide died for their faith. Are we mourning?

On a daily basis our brothers and sisters who are church leaders in the Two-Thirds World struggle with poverty, war, disease and corruption that is a way of life. Do we help share their burden? The distance that separates us is merely geographical but the brother-hood that unites us is spiritual and God-given. Justice and mercy are a central aspect of God's mission, and the responsibility of his children.

Jesus said, 'My mother and brothers are those who hear God's word and put it into practice.'

Father,
thank you that you have made me your child,
that I am adopted into your family:
remind me that my spiritual brothers and sisters are your
    children too,
that your family is worldwide,
and that my responsibility for them should impact my life,
whether they are on the other side of the table
    or on the other side of the world.

Day 33

WEEK 5: OPENING OUR HEARTS TO SUFFERING

ANDREW McLELLAN

The Son of Man must suffer
Luke 9:18–27

He must be killed and on the third day be raised to life.
(Luke 9:22)

The Son of Man must undergo great suffering. If the title 'Son of Man' were to mean that Jesus is *the* human being, the most human of all humans, then this would be a true sentence. Undergoing great suffering is part of the human condition. Despite appearances, it is what life involves for everyone. It is no surprise if the representative human being must undergo great suffering.

Curiously, that can be a helpful thing to remember. Helpful when the world seems desperately unfair, when it looks as if everyone else is getting through life without the blows which we have to deal with. It is also right to remember it, to remember that suffering is part of life for everyone: in school, in family, in church. Christian Aid knows all too well about the suffering which millions upon millions must face. Hunger and disease are their daily lot. In the countries and cities of the headlines and in unnumbered forgotten villages all across the poor world, Christian Aid is at work. In these suffering children of God, still the Son of Man must undergo great suffering.

Suffering is certainly the human situation in prisons. Different people have different views about what prisons should be like; but there should be no doubt in the minds of anyone that in reality prisons are, and always have been, places of great suffering. Sometimes it can be tasted in the first few minutes inside a prison; sometimes it is hidden. But always prisons are places of pain and ugliness and great suffering. That means for Christians that prisons are places for which God has a special care: in them, still, the Son of Man must undergo great suffering.

The title 'Son of Man', however, for most Bible scholars, means something different from a title of Jesus as the true human being. It is a way of speaking about Jesus the Messiah. The sufferings in this part of the gospel story are the sufferings of the one who is to fulfil the purposes of God for all the world. In pain he offers himself and in pain his body is broken for us. In his sufferings God is incarnate, made flesh. This week sees the Son of Man moving towards his exaltation as we watch Jesus moving towards his crucifixion.

God my friend, I give you thanks for the most human life of Jesus. He struggled as I struggle; he knew weakness as I know weakness; he was tempted as I am tempted. But he believed as I never have; he loved as I never could; he suffered as I never will: to win for me healing and forgiveness and life in all its fullness.

Day 34

Breaking the rules
Luke 13:10–17

Should not this woman . . . be set free on the Sabbath day from what bound her? (Luke 13:16)

When Jesus heals a woman on the Sabbath day, those who see it are quite clear that he is breaking the law. How will a story about Jesus breaking the law sound in prison?

Most prisoners will never hear it: reading the Bible and attending worship are decidedly minority activities in all British jails. Nevertheless, some Christian prisoners do continue to practise their religion, and regularly there are moving stories of people coming to faith in prison.

Perhaps some prisoners will say, 'It was different for him.' All of us say that sometimes about Jesus. As if he didn't feel the pain because he was Jesus; as if he didn't bleed when he was flogged, didn't suffer agony when he was crucified. If it was different for Jesus it was different because he loved his enemies and wept for their wrong; because he trusted in God and still found the world full of pain. If it was different for Jesus it was different because the suffering was worse.

Some prisoners might say, 'Just like me', particularly prisoners who know that they have been imprisoned for what they have believed: for it was because of his convictions about God and human beings that people plotted the arrest and execution of Jesus. Political prisoners are to be found in every continent. Their cause ought to be the cause of the followers of Jesus.

There might just be one or two prisoners who read of Jesus being attacked and then crucified for breaking the law and then say, 'I deserve what has happened to me: he did not.' That is the thought of one of the thieves crucified beside Jesus. If any prisoners read the story of the suffering of Jesus in that way then they will be teaching us all. For that is an old and holy way, perhaps the only way for Christians to read about the suffering of Jesus. 'I deserved it, he did not.' *He was pierced for our transgressions, he was crushed for our iniquities; the punishment that brought us peace was upon him, and by his wounds we are healed.*

Jesus is present with outstretched arms shining with light: in my darkness he is giving me light. Jesus is present with arms outstretched in love: in my anxiety he is giving me love. Jesus is present with outstretched arms full of power: in my weakness he is offering me strength.

Day 35

The great weight of sin
Luke 5:17–26

Friend, your sins are forgiven. (Luke 5:20)

In this story the Pharisees have more spiritual insight than most modern readers. Most modern readers find it a difficult story because they think that making someone get up and walk must be more difficult than forgiving someone's sins. At least the Pharisees understand how immensely difficult the forgiveness of sins might be, how very costly. The most famous English theologian, St Anselm, is remembered for a warning to those who have not yet considered 'how great is the weight of sin'.

Some things are more clear in prison. There are stories there of terrible things: terrible things done to children, to women; terrible things done for drugs; deliberate, exploitative cruelty. It is not easy to spend much time in prison without becoming aware of 'how great is the weight of sin'. If the Christian faith is true, then God is able to forgive even these things: and that might be more wonderful than making a lame man get up and walk.

That can have a personal meaning. If the Christian faith is true, God is able to forgive me. Most people who think about these things at all are a curious mixture. On the one hand dismissive about sin – like the readers of this story who think that it is easy to forgive sins – on the other hand full of low self-esteem and feelings of unworthiness which make guilt and shame companions who never disappear. Readers who begin to understand this story recognise their own faces in the face of the man brought by his friends to Jesus.

Primarily, however, this is a story about Jesus, and about the mystery of Jesus. In all of the Gospels where it appears, this story of healing the man who cannot walk is one of the first signs of opposition. As the darkness of his punishment first casts its shadow across the gospel story, the strangeness of his wrongdoing becomes clear. He heals and he forgives – and then the plotting begins.

> *Why, what hath my Lord done?*
> *What makes this rage and spite?*
> *He made the lame to run,*
> *He gave the blind their sight.*
> *Sweet injuries!*
> *Yet they at these*
> *Themselves displease,*
> *And 'gainst him rise.*
>
> (Samuel Crossman)

I have come to find wisdom. I have come to find strength. I have come to find forgiveness. I have come to find peace. I have come to find love. I have come to find the healing and forgiveness one man found when his friends brought him to Jesus.

Day 36

A grieving mother
Luke 7:11–17

When the Lord saw her, his heart went out to her.
(Luke 7:13)

One of the most depressing prison statistics is this: compared with the population as a whole, prisoners are fourteen times more likely to have been taken into care as children. It is much less likely that a prisoner will have grown up knowing a mother's care, a mother's smile, a mother's tears, a mother's prayer. For children a mother's love can be a powerful source of healing and tenderness, and its absence can be so very damaging. Many young offenders have no experience whatever of being loved.

Jesus meets a weeping mother. She is grieving for her only son. While many prisoners have known very little love, many have families outside. For them life can be bitter. For some the prisoner is ever-present in the heart: the desolation felt in the lonely cell is felt as painfully by those who care outside. For some the difficulties of balancing other family responsibilities and visiting and getting by on a tiny budget can be overwhelming. For some, especially the families of sex offenders, there is a daily fear of public reaction. Families outside weep as well.

Jesus meets a woman in tears and has compassion on her. The story copies quite closely an Old Testament story of Elijah and a widow's son (1 Kings 17:17–24); but one of the differences is that the Gospel writers specifically insert 'compassion' as the motive for responding to the widow's need. For those who follow Jesus there is something quite fundamental about responding to the suffering of others with compassion. It is fundamental because it is the way of Jesus. Christian Aid is driven by seeking justice and healing and peace and feeding the hungry, all of which mark the Jesus of the Gospels; but it is also and always driven by compassion.

What makes this a difficult story is that it is a story of life given back to a dead person. There are only three such stories in the Gospels before the Easter story, and this one is perhaps the most elusive. Let it be a hint of the power of God over all that seeks to destroy human life, the power of God over the most intense suffering. And let it also be a reminder of the most enduring of Christian Aid slogans: *we believe in life before death.*

Lord of Life in the kingdom of death, use my prayers to bring life. To bring life before death to a hungry world; where sick people lie around outside hospitals because there is no room inside; where parents watch helplessly as their children die. Use my prayers and use me to bring life.

Day 37

The outcast
Luke 8:26–39

He had . . . been driven by the demon into solitary places.
(Luke 8:29)

Mental illness arouses fear and hostility today as it did in the time of Jesus. Once in Canada I noticed a man on a seat in the sun on a pavement where many busy people were hurrying past. Without exception people steered away from the seat as they came near, for they saw that he was clearly disturbed. Without exception, for I did the same. Just at that moment a pretty girl coming the other way stopped beside him. She asked if she might sit down, and she began chatting to him. I am not sure if it was a wise thing to do, but it had some of the authentic marks of Jesus of Nazareth.

It takes only a very little thinking to realise that mental illness is spread across every section of every society. In the very poorest countries of the world, depression and anxiety and schizophrenia abound: people do not escape from psychiatric illness just because they are poor. Some of the most important medical aid the poor world needs is the kind of aid which treats illnesses which are unseen.

The Bible says 'perfect love drives out fear'. In story after story Jesus stands with those who make everyone else afraid. Prostitutes and people with leprosy and sufferers from mental illness may not have much in common; but all of them made (and often make) others afraid. Over and over again Jesus stands with them. Not only does he stand with them: he gives them their lives back again, with the painful places healed.

There are many, many people with mental illness in our prisons. Compared with the population as a whole, prisoners are fifty times more likely to suffer from three or more mental disorders. The governor of a huge London prison has described his job as 'managing the largest secure psychiatric unit in Europe'. Of course, many should not be in prison, but prison is where they are. For healthy people it can be terrifying to come into prison: for those who are not able to react or to relate in normal ways it can be excruciatingly awful. It is always good to pray for prisoners, the outcasts of society. Sometimes it is good to remember those prisoners with mental illness, outcasts from a community of outcasts.

Let me be the voice of those whose minds are weak, in the dark night of depression or mental disturbance; those in old age who can no longer remember the words, nor who they are, nor those who love them. Let my prayer be the voice of those for whom the business of living is too much to grasp. Hear my prayer.

Day 38

The incurable
Luke 8:42b–7

*She told why she had touched him and how she had been
instantly healed. (Luke 8:47)*

Nearly every woman Jesus meets is a suffering woman. This is
no accident: the New Testament writers are proclaiming that
the kingdom of God is coming upon those who have no hope. It is
a message that women in prison desperately need to hear.

For nearly all prisoners who are women are themselves victims.
Most prisoners are in some sense victims. To say this is not to
diminish the horrific nature of some crimes, nor to undervalue the
suffering, the apparently endless suffering, of the victims of some
crimes. It is simply to recognise the fact that most prisoners have
had bad experiences of life and in particular bad experiences at the
hands of other human beings. Almost every female prisoner, however, is a victim. As well as being the victim of the cruel forces
which have attacked male prisoners, like poverty and violence and
addiction, she is nearly always a victim of men. Occasionally prisons
for women manage to produce some cheerfulness; for all that, they
are perhaps the most painful places in the land.

Jesus meets a woman whose pain has lasted for fourteen years. She
seeks healing from him, and she seeks it in secret. But Jesus wants to
know her, to identify her, to meet her. This looks strange, for what
effect can her identification have except to bring embarrassment?
Jesus does want to meet her, and he wants to meet her so that he can
say to her, 'Daughter, your faith has healed you. Go in peace.' He
wants her whole life, and not only her body, to be blessed.

All the poor suffer, but all across the world women suffer most. In nearly every poor society, women eat last; so women eat what, if anything, is left. United Nations statistics make clear that women are half the world's population, do two-thirds of the world's work, earn one-tenth of the world's income and own less than one-hundredth of the world's property. Fighting for justice for all the world's poor often means fighting in particular for justice for women.

May my prayer for women be a prayer for love. Love when they have known violence instead of tenderness; love when they have known rejection instead of acceptance; love when they have known hurt instead of healing. My prayer for them is for the love of God.

Day 39

The beggar
Luke 16:19–31

Lazarus [was] covered with sores and longing to eat what fell from the rich man's table. (Luke 16:20–1)

Jesus tells a story about a rich man and a poor man. Like several parables, and despite the views of the great Bible critics of an earlier day, it is a story with more than one point. But it is at least a story about denying food to the poor. Put your money where your mouth is. Put your money where his mouth is. The dangers of wealth is such a characteristic theme for Luke.

Over the last few years a biblical idea of jubilee has inspired the churches and the whole world together to demand the cancellation of unrepayable debt. The relations between the world's rich and the world's poor are judged by a story Jesus told about a rich man and a poor man: and by the past and present determination of those of us who are rich to grab all we can, and more, from the mouths of the poor.

The suffering of the poor – that is what Christian aid agencies are about. Relieving the suffering of the poor, putting a stop to their suffering.

Overwhelmingly, prison populations are made up of poor people. Compared with the population as a whole, prisoners are five times more likely to have no educational qualification, twelve times more likely to have experienced long-term unemployment, thirty times more likely to be homeless. The story about the rich man and Lazarus is a story about how invisible poor people are. By definition, the poor people who are in prison are completely invisible, but that does not mean they are to be ignored or forgotten. Of course, they can be ignored or forgotten: but Jesus told this story so that those who are his friends might learn.

As Holy Week approaches and the sufferings of Jesus are spread wide on the cross, it is right to remember his strong words – among the hardest recorded in the Gospels – about the sufferings of the poor. He was one of them himself, and their sufferings are his sufferings still. *The Son of Man must undergo great suffering.*

Let me weep today with the poor. With those in our great cities where the happiness of so many homes is fragile. With the poor of a hungry world, where endless labour brings no riches. Let me weep and work and pray for the day when God will wipe away every tear.

HOLY WEEK: OPENING OUR HEARTS IN LOVE

LAVINIA BYRNE

Weeping for the city
Luke 19:28–44

They . . . threw their cloaks on the colt and put Jesus on it.
As he went along, people spread their cloaks on the road.
(Luke 19:35–6)

Holy Week opens with Palm Sunday. The drama of the final week of the life of Jesus begins. We go with him to his Passion and so the last redemptive events of this sacred week engage us freshly, as they do each year.

This year, though, they have a special resonance for us, for our world seems more than ever to need redemption from all kinds of malaise and threat. So a poignant and telling question for every disciple: are we to be spectators, watching safely from afar, wrapped up in our own concerns and those of our world? Or are we to be participants in the sufferings of our Saviour?

Take up a role in the Passion drama. Today, as Jesus enters Jerusalem, decide what you are going to be. The colt, who has never been ridden and yet who will bear Jesus into the holy city? A cloak, randomly thrown to make a seat on which he may ride? Or thrown on to the ground, along with palm leaves? The path, which brings him inexorably to his destiny? Or a voice in the crowd, somehow much less functional, but louder, as you cry, 'Blessed is the King'?

Remember, though, the perils of that option. For crowds are fickle and your praise of God may die on your lips if, later in the week, you find yourself calling out for the life of Barabbas to be preserved over that of your Lord.

Go with him now into Jerusalem. Hear the roar of the crowd. Smell the smells. Experience the sense of hope and the omens of doom. Follow the leadings of the Holy Spirit and offer yourself to be with him in what will happen here. As you do so, remember that 'Christ will be in agony until the end of the world', as Pascal said. And that there are people the world over who could do with a donkey, a cloak, a flourishing palm tree, a new path. To engage with the Passion of Jesus is to engage with their suffering too. Open your heart to the events of this week. Let it be different for you.

Lord Jesus Christ, as you follow the leadings of the Holy Spirit and make your way to Jerusalem, help us to be there with you. Give us small and functional tasks in the story of salvation and help us to fulfil them for the true and certain glory and praise of your name. Amen.

Day 41

Death of a loved son
Luke 20:9–17

I will send my son, whom I love; perhaps they
will respect him. (Luke 20:13)

What then does this text mean? How do you situate yourself in the story? Imagine first that you are a tenant farmer. Not necessarily a good person but, there again, not a bad one either. Imagine you are the vineyard. Sitting there on the hillside, basking in the sun yet requiring clever stewardship, a good owner and a vine grower who knows how to tend you adequately. Imagine you are the first slave, the second slave or a messenger who gets no sense out of anyone.

If you are the vineyard you are now part of a great drama, because people with apparently conflicting interests are battling over you. Yet there appears to be a breakthrough moment, for the son and heir of the man who first planted you comes to you as well. A real conversation is possible. There is hope. But, if you are one of these tenant farmers, what do you choose to do? To talk among yourselves. To set your own agenda. To protect your own assets.

In this way, as Jesus taught, self-interest prevails. And, of course, there are casualties, and the first of these is the Son of God himself. Holy Week offers us the opportunity to open our hearts, to widen our frame of reference, to acknowledge that the good of the wider human project is more important than our own narrow concerns.

Rejection is such an easy option – the easiest of all, really. Rejection means blocking our ears from hearing the good news; rejection means setting our backs to strangers who come from outside; rejection means assessing people in terms of their social status – as slaves or sons – and treating them accordingly.

Whereas the health of the whole project of vine-growing is all about recognition, and it involves acknowledging the needs of the vineyard and the rights of the master of the vineyard, who is Lord of us all.

Today, Lord, we pray for eyes to see and ears to hear. Take away our fear, set the peace of heaven in our hearts so that we may recognise you, the Master who first planted the vineyard, in the humblest and most exalted of the tasks you ask us to do. Give us the grace to listen to you at all times, however painful the message. Amen.

Day 42

A mother faces loss
Luke 2:22–38

A sword will pierce your own soul too. (Luke 2:35)

As a young woman, Mary, the mother of Jesus, took her child to the temple in Jerusalem to present him to the Lord and to fulfil the requirements of the law. Two people met them there. We recall Simeon and Anna, who began to praise God and to say that redemption was at hand. But Simeon had a warning for Mary – ominous words that troubled those who heard them, for the language is graphic. It associates Mary in a very particular way with the sufferings of her son.

Different bits of the Christian church have struggled to know how to understand the words of Simeon and the understanding they offer of Mary's role in her son's suffering. On the one hand, there are those who have tried to excise Mary from the Christian imagination because they assumed that she was getting too close and that any attempt to offer her more of a place than that of any other Christian follower would somehow take away from the importance of her son. On the other, there are those who domesticated her, turned her into some kind of generic mother, who would sort us out like naughty children. Both forgot the insights of the Council of Ephesus, which declared that Mary was the mother of God and commended her to us as a figure of faith, someone whom we can invoke to intercede for, to pray for, our troubled world.

Why should she care? Well, for the very reason that she stood at the foot of the cross and that she received the battered body of her son into her arms. That is what we are recalling today.

So how had Mary been prepared? Simeon gave the warning and the young mother herself was 'treasur[ing] up all these things in her heart'. Is that the secret? That prayerful reflection enables you to understand things, even the worse things of all, like the death of your own child, the collapse of a spiritual vision, total heartbreak?

Mary, the mother of Jesus, stands at the foot of the cross and watches him die. Her heart and her soul are pierced to the quick. Perhaps that is why the oldest Marian prayer from the Christian tradition ends with these words: '*Holy Mary, mother of God, pray for us sinners, now and at the hour of our death.*'

For reflection:

> *Mary said:*
> '*My soul glorifies the Lord*
> *and my spirit rejoices in God my Saviour,*
> *for he has been mindful*
> *of the humble state of his servant.*
> *From now on all generations will call me blessed,*
> *for the Mighty One has done great things for me –*
> *holy is his name.*'
>
> *(Luke 2:46–9)*

Day 43

Love and the kingdom
Luke 22:24–30

A dispute arose among them as to which of them was considered to be greatest. (Luke 22:24)

Spy Wednesday. The pace changes as we move into the final few days of Holy Week. Judas is preparing his betrayal and all the signs that Jesus warned of are falling into place. The drama is played out in the outer world but also in our own inner worlds as well. Different bits of ourselves war on each other as our interior sun, moon and stars, our seas and our waves re-constellate.

We believe that the Son of Man will come again. Yet while we await his return, we do well to reflect on the tumult of the Passion narrative, for it opens our hearts to insight, as well as love. Two characters in particular offer us a mirror today: Judas, after whom Spy Wednesday is named, and Peter.

Think of Peter and Judas, and don't simply think of them now, when they look disaster in the face. Remember them at the beginning, when they first set out to be disciples. When Jesus first called them, did they like each other? Did they get on? They were both part of the inner group, the close circle of friends, the apostles. Peter the fisherman, Judas who kept the purse. Both drawn inexorably together. We see them by the shore of the Sea of Galilee, watch them as they wander through the grain fields or go up to listen to the Sermon on the Mount. Driven by the dynamic of the kingdom of God which Jesus spoke about, where the pure and the meek would inherit the earth. They aspired to be like that. That was their dream and the months they first spent following Jesus were their dreamtime.

Now, of course, we know that it all fell apart. The dénouement we recall during Holy Week is chilling. For Judas sold Jesus for thirty pieces of silver and then went out to hang himself, whereas Peter seemed to stand by Jesus and then denied him three times. Neither proved to be either pure or meek. Neither stood to inherit the earth, let alone to gain the eternal life to which they had once aspired.

Lord Jesus Christ, confirm your choice of us, even when we fail you. We know you judge us more leniently than we judge ourselves. Give us the grace to pick ourselves up – like Peter – when we fail; protect us from the despair which overcame Judas. Amen.

Day 44: Maundy Thursday

Responding to betrayal
Luke 22:47–53

Jesus . . . touched the man's ear and healed him.
(Luke 22:51)

The desire to heal is profound and of the essence of the Christian calling. Today we remember that Jesus reached out to touch and heal one of the very men who came to arrest him. He met violence with love.

On Maundy Thursday, as we consider his response to betrayal, we also recall the final meal that Jesus shared with his friends: the moment when he chose to give his body and blood for the salvation of the world; the moment when he offered us a meal that was to be for ultimate healing.

A graced moment when he sat at table with his friends and spoke to them from his heart. Everything he had been for them was to be pulled together in an act of sharing that was intended to be life-giving and therefore to be repeated in his name.

The Eucharist offers us a way of exploring our discipleship. For the Gospel accounts of the Last Supper supply us with a collection of pictures. Jesus took bread, blessed it, broke it and gave it. Each of these is a healing gesture and each was to be replicated.

So when we first hear the call to discipleship, we too are taken, chosen, set apart by God's call. Then we are blessed with the gift of baptism and the recognition it represents as we become members of the family of Christ. True discipleship means following a suffering Lord, so in turn we are broken and shared for the life of the world. Discipleship is costly because it demands our all.

The pattern offered by Jesus is counter-cultural. Ours is a society that loves to take and break, to have and to use and then to discard. What we learn from the healing ministry of Jesus is that even the fragments should be gathered up. Nothing is wasted. Right up to the moment of his arrest, Jesus continued to teach us through his actions. So we need to attend when he heals his enemy. The ear of the servant of the High Priest was healed so that he could witness and listen to the events that unfolded in front of him. His ear was healed so that we in turn should be attentive and not miss a detail of what was going on as Jesus faced up to the people who wanted him destroyed.

Lord Jesus Christ, lover of life, heal us now as we too come to you in our hour of need. Help us to hear your call so that we may be taken, blessed, broken and given in the service of your holy name. Amen.

Day 45: Good Friday

Dying strangers
Luke 23:39–43

Jesus, remember me when you come into your kingdom.
(Luke 23:42)

And so we come to the cross and find that we are not alone, because Jesus does not die on his own. Symbolically he is portrayed hanging between two other people. And they, in some strange way, represent bits of ourselves. The crucifixion scene offers a mirror to us. On one side, a thief who blasphemes him. Someone who is deaf to the evidence that stares him in the face. On the other side, another criminal, yet one who recognises the goodness of his Saviour and who prays to join him in paradise.

We recognise this scenario because it is one that is lived out in our own lives. We are constantly torn by the dilemma of attraction and revulsion displayed for us in the crucifixion. We are not comfortable as we take our stand at the foot of the cross. We know, for example, that we are sinners, however confident we are in the redemption that has been enacted for us here. We know that we are thieves and cheats and liars; that we compromise with the truth; that we are not worthy.

So sometimes we rebel and choose to live out the dark side of our nature, rejecting the love and forgiveness that Jesus offers us. We reject our salvation. At other times, like the good thief, we turn to him in the confidence that we will be with him in paradise because we are 'ransomed, healed, restored, forgiven'.

As we stand at the foot of the cross, we reflect on our betrayals and we recall our experiences of forgiveness. We pray to be like the good thief, the man who accepted redemption at the hand of Jesus.

So how are we to do this? The Gospel offers a suggestion by insisting that the good thief knew that he was under judgment. He acknowledged that he had done wrong and that is why he could be forgiven and accept the fruits of forgiveness. The other thief denied that there was anything the matter. If we accept our own vulnerability and transgressions, if we have the simplicity and humility to say, 'I am sorry; I have done wrong; I need you', we will find that we turn to a Saviour who has already opened the gates of paradise to us and whose will and purpose is that we should join him there.

> *Lord Jesus Christ, today we stand at the foot of the cross and wait with you there. As we open the gates of our hearts to you in love, open the gates of paradise to us and to your world. Amen.*

Day 46: Holy Saturday

Love beyond death
Luke 23:50–6

The women . . . went home and prepared spices and perfumes. (Luke 23:56)

Holy Saturday. The Sabbath. A day of rest. After the rigours of Good Friday, today we could be forgiven for standing aside from the mysteries and rituals of Holy Week. Yet there is a further task for us and we cannot sit back and wallow in our sense of loss at what has happened. Nor can we move forward a day and bask in the glory of our redemption. For in the new dispensation, the one that Jesus initiated by dying for our salvation, today is set to become a day of transformation. Indeed, the Christian tradition, while acknowledging Jesus' death and departure from us, nevertheless talks about his activity on this strange day and proposes that we too should see it as a day of presence rather than of absence, a day of preparation.

So what happens? Joseph of Arimathea, the good and righteous man who was waiting for the kingdom of God, went and asked Pilate for the body of Jesus so that he could bury him honourably. The women came to visit the tomb and prepared their spices and ointments to anoint him. Jesus too is presented to us in medieval architecture and iconography, as well as in the literature of mystery plays, with a special role on this day. He visits the bodies of the saints who languish as they wait for redemption and, in his 'harrowing of hell', frees them to go to eternal life in heaven. Similarly, we too have a task on Holy Saturday. Our parents in faith are released from the emptiness of perdition to the fullness of redemption.

How can we engage with this mystery? Where can we find something that is apparently dead? Where can we find a friendship that we have neglected, a person whom we have ignored, a cause that we have abandoned? How can we find these and call them back to life? Today is a day for engaging with the dead, for letting go of what we cannot bring back to life and a day for preparing spices and ointments, seeking out opportunities for helping life come back into our lives. Today we need to harrow our own hells and bring life where there was only death.

Heavenly Father, today you waited as your holy Son went down among the dead. Grant us a day of preparation as we try to understand how we can bring life back to dead friendships, empty relationships and abandoned causes. Prepare us for the new life you offer through the power of the Spirit in your Son, Jesus Christ, our Lord. Amen.

Day 47: Easter Sunday

Resurrection love
Luke 24:35–49

Look at my hands and my feet. (Luke 24:39)

On Easter Sunday, Jesus offers us the gift of presence and the gift of peace.

We are to know him in the breaking of the bread. Jesus does not want to be insubstantial; he does not want to be a ghost. Instead he comes to us and invites us to touch him. He offers himself to us in ways that are intended to nourish and nurture us. He promises companionship.

So where are we to touch him in today's world? Where are we to walk with him? Where are we to find his hands and feet? Where are we to offer him a piece of broiled fish and eat and drink in his presence? Christianity is an embodied religion. It does not live between the pages of a book. Rather, it invites us to engage with our world. So we are to recognise the presence of Jesus whenever there are wounded hands and feet that turn to us for healing and wherever there is a road that we can walk down in his company.

The gift lies in recognising him even when he presents himself to us in hidden and unexpected ways. We need to believe that we can touch him in our everyday lives. We need to understand that we can walk with him. Our task is to seek out people who are needy and to turn our faces towards them rather than away from them. This is not difficult to do, for there are many wounded hands and feet that clamour for our attention. There are many hungry people who would love a bowl of fish, let alone a loaf of bread.

If Jesus is risen from the dead then we need proof, we need evidence. How can we secure this in today's world? The gospel seems to suggest that the way forward is to open our hearts in love. No one is to be excluded, no situation is beyond the reach of grace. By believing this and by putting it into practice, we can become witnesses and carry the echo of his saving mission forwards into our world. Christian faith is not a personal possession. It is always for sharing. So everything comes full circle. We can be his witnesses. We can provide the evidence that he is risen.

We pray with the words of a prayer written by Teresa of Avila:

Christ has no body now on earth but yours, no hands but yours, no feet but yours; yours are the eyes through which to look at Christ's compassion to the world, yours are the feet with which he is to go about doing good, and yours are the hands with which he is to bless us now. Amen.

Notes

1   Quotation from Robert Van de Weyer, *The Illustrated Book of Christian Literature* (Arthur James, 1998), p. 20.
2   Quotation from Michael Taylor, *Poverty and Christianity: Reflections at the Interface between Faith and Experience* (SCM Press, 2000), p. 124.